AUTOMOBILES

Connecting People and Places

These and other books are included in the
Encyclopedia of Discovery and Invention series:

Airplanes
Anesthetics
Animation
Atoms
Automobiles
Clocks
Computers
Genetics
Germs
Gravity
Guns
Human Origins
Lasers
Microscopes

Movies
Phonograph
Photography
Plate Tectonics
Printing Press
Radar
Radios
Railroads
Ships
Submarines
Telephones
Telescopes
Television
Vaccines

AUTOMOBILES
Connecting People and Places

by MYRA H. IMMELL

The ENCYCLOPEDIA of
D·I·S·C·O·V·E·R·Y
and **INVENTION**

P.O. Box 289011 SAN DIEGO, CA 92198-9011

Library of Congress Cataloging-in-Publication Data

Immell, Myra H.,
  Automobiles: connecting people and places / by Myra H.
Immell.

    p. cm.—(The Encyclopedia of discovery and invention)
  Includes bibliographical references and index.
  Summary: Traces the development of the automobile and
its effects on civilization over time.
  ISBN 1-56006-226-6 (acid-free paper)
  1. Automobiles—History—Juvenile literature.
[1. Automobiles.]   I. Title.   II. Series.
TL206.I46   1994
629.222'09—dc20   93-4553
                                                 CIP
                                                 AC

Contents

■■■

Foreword

The belief in progress has been one of the dominant forces in Western Civilization from the Scientific Revolution of the seventeenth century to the present. Embodied in the idea of progress is the conviction that each generation will be better off than the one that preceded it. Eventually, all peoples will benefit from and share in this better world. R.R. Palmer, in his *History of the Modern World*, calls this belief in progress "a kind of nonreligious faith that the conditions of human life" will continually improve as time goes on.

For over a thousand years prior to the seventeenth century, science had progressed little. Inquiry was largely discouraged, and experimentation, almost nonexistent. As a result, science became regressive and discovery was ignored. Benjamin Farrington, a historian of science, characterized it this way: "Science had failed to become a real force in the life of society. Instead there had arisen a conception of science as a cycle of liberal studies for a privileged minority. Science ceased to be a means of transforming the conditions of life." In short, had this intellectual climate continued, humanity's future would have been little more than a clone of its past.

Fortunately, these circumstances were not destined to last. By the seventeenth and eighteenth centuries, Western society was undergoing radical and favorable changes. And the changes that occurred gave rise to the notion that progress was a real force urging civilization forward. Surpluses of consumer goods were replacing substandard living conditions in most of Western Europe. Rigid class systems were giving way to social mobility. In nations like France and the United States, the lofty principles of democracy and popular sovereignty were being painted in broad, gilded strokes over the fading canvasses of monarchy and despotism.

But more significant than these social, economic, and political changes, the new age witnessed a rebirth of science. Centuries of scientific stagnation began crumbling before a spirit of scientific inquiry that spawned undreamed of technological advances. And it was the discoveries and inventions of scores of men and women that fueled these new technologies, dramatically increasing the ability of humankind to control nature—and, many believed, eventually to guide it.

It is a truism of science and technology that the results derived from observation and experimentation are not finalities. They are part of a process. Each discovery is but one piece in a continuum bridging past and present and heralding an extraordinary future. The heroic age of the Scientific Revolution was simply a start. It laid a foundation upon which succeeding generations of imaginative thinkers could build. It kindled the belief that progress is possible as long as there were gifted men and women who would respond to society's needs. When Antonie van Leeuwenhoek observed *Animalcules* (little animals) through his high-powered microscope in 1683, the discovery did not end there. Others followed who would call these "little animals" bacteria and, in time, recognize their role in the process of health and disease. Robert Koch, a German bacteriologist and winner of the Nobel Prize in Physiology and Medicine, was one of these men. Koch firmly established that bacteria are responsible for causing infectious diseases. He identified, among others, the causative organisms of anthrax and tuberculosis. Alexander Fleming, another Nobel Laureate, progressed still further in the quest to understand and control bacteria. In 1928, Fleming discovered penicillin, the antibiotic wonder drug. Penicillin, and the generations of antibiotics that succeeded it, have done more to

prevent premature death than any other discovery in the history of humankind. And as civilization hastens toward the twenty-first century, most agree that the conquest of van Leeuwenhoek's "little animals" will continue.

The *Encyclopedia of Discovery and Invention* examines those discoveries and inventions that have had a sweeping impact on life and thought in the modern world. Each book explores the ideas that led to the invention or discovery, and, more importantly, how the world changed and continues to change because of it. The series also highlights the people behind the achievements—the unique men and women whose singular genius and rich imagination have altered the lives of everyone. Enhanced by photographs and clearly explained technical drawings, these books are comprehensive examinations of the building blocks of human progress.

AUTOMOBILES

Connecting People and Places

AUTOMOBILES

Introduction

In the late 1800s, a new word was used for the first time in France. That word was *automobile*. Then as now, the word referred to a wheeled land vehicle that produces its own power and is subject only to the will of the driver.

No one person invented the automobile. It evolved over time to fulfill the need for a more efficient form of transport. People wanted a vehicle that could carry them and their goods with little or no effort on their part. The word itself comes from the languages of two different countries—it is a combination of the Greek word *auto*, which means "self," and the French word *mobile*, which means "moving."

The dream that such a vehicle could exist really began with the invention of the wheel. That was more than 5,000 years ago. Over time, the dream led to new and improved means of land transport. One of these was the automobile.

The automobile changed people's lives for all time, providing unprecedented opportunities. Many of the things we do routinely or take for granted today were not possible before the automobile. Because of the automobile, roads were built where none had existed. These roads connected people and places.

... TIMELINE: AUTOMOBILES

1 2 3 4 5 6 7 8 9 10

1 ■ 150 B.C.
Hero of Alexandria builds the *aeolipile*, the world's first primitive steam engine.

2 ■ 1672
Father Ferdinand Verbiest builds a small-scale cart driven by a steam engine.

3 ■ 1769
Captain Nicholas Joseph Cugnot builds the first full-scale, steam-propelled road vehicle.

4 ■ 1800
Richard Trevithick invents a high-pressure steam engine and uses it the following year to propel a carriage.

5 ■ 1805
Oliver Evans demonstrates his steam-propelled amphibious dredge, *Orukter Amphibolos*.

6 ■ 1839
Robert Anderson, a Scot, builds the first crude electric car.

7 ■ 1862
Jean Joseph Etienne Lenoir proves that his two-stroke internal combustion engine can propel a vehicle.

8 ■ 1876
Nicolaus August Otto patents the four-stroke internal combustion engine, Silent Otto.

9 ■ 1885
Karl Benz creates the first practical automobile powered by an internal combustion engine.

10 ■ 1886
Gottlieb Daimler produces the first automobile powered by a high-speed internal combustion engine.

11 ■ 1890
William Morrison of Des Moines, Iowa, becomes the first person to manufacture and sell an electric car.

12 ■ 1893
Charles E. and J. Frank Duryea produce the "buggynaut," America's first internal combustion car.

With each improvement in the automobile came more change for humankind. People became more and more mobile, able to travel near and far more easily and faster. Also because of the automobile, some industries and businesses faded or disappeared and new industries and businesses came into being. This, in turn, led to the creation of new kinds of jobs. For many people, this meant a new, different way of life, often in a place far from their hometown.

The automobile continues to impact our lives today. Without the automobile, many people who live in one place and work in another might have no way to travel quickly and inexpensively between home and job. And what about all the people worldwide who work in the automobile industry, the travel industry, or other automobile-related industries? They depend on the automobile for their livelihoods.

Present-day engineers, inventors, and scientists are well aware of the automobile's role and importance. They are equally aware of the lives the automobile has taken and the environmental problems it has caused. For this reason, men and women of vision all over the world are working—and will go on working—to produce automobiles that are safer for us and for the environment.

11 ▷ 12 ▷ 13 ▷ 14 ▷ 15 ▷ 16 ▷   17 ▷ 18 ▷ 19 ▷   20 ▷ 21 ▷ 22 ▷

13 ■ 1897
F.E. and F.O. Stanley produce the original Stanley Steamer.

14 ■ 1901
The Mercedes, the first real luxury car, is unveiled in Nice, France.

15 ■ 1908
Henry M. Leland of Cadillac produces the first automobiles with interchangeable parts; Henry Ford introduces the "universal automobile," the Model T.

16 ■ 1912
Cadillac introduces the electric starter; Henry Ford revolutionizes the assembly line process.

17 ■ 1930
Middle-class families in Europe start buying cars for the first time.

18 ■ 1945
The Volkswagen "Beetle" is introduced and gives many German families their first chance to go driving.

19 ■ 1954
The Wankel rotary engine is introduced.

20 ■ 1980
A Japanese manufacturer, Toyota, becomes the leading seller of cars in the United States.

21 ■ 1985
Most cars have systems with full or partial control by computer.

22 ■ 1990
California passes a law that encourages automakers to develop automobiles powered by electricity or by an alternative fuel.

23 ■ 1992
A sophisticated operation—TravTek—involving "smart" cars and "smart" highways is tested in the United States.

Once upon a Wheel

The automobile did not appear overnight. It evolved over centuries as creative people in different parts of the world tried to fulfill the dream of a self-moving vehicle. To power the machines they created, they used everything from the forces of nature to a giant clock spring to a kind of funnel with a cork in it.

Many of the early driving machines were fantastic sources of wonder to the peoples of the time. But not until enterprising men learned how to harness the power of steam did any of these devices meet with real success.

The Power of Steam

Ancient peoples who lived before the birth of Christ recognized that steam could be used to move objects. Legend has it, for example, that in 800 B.C. the Chinese created "fire carts" propelled by steam. Then there were the Greeks. In an epic poem called the *Iliad*, the ancient Greek poet Homer told how the fire god Hephaestus—known as Vulcan to the Romans—built three-wheeled vehicles that rolled from place to place under their own power. Through trade, the Greeks probably spread their knowledge about steam across southern Europe and northern Africa.

Still later—around 150 B.C.—the mathematician Hero of Alexandria built a device called the *aeolipile.* Thought to be the world's first primitive steam engine, it worked this way. A fire was kept lit under a bowllike boiler to generate steam. The steam passed upward through hollow tubes into a hollow ball. Across from each other on the ball were two nozzles. As the steam escaped through the nozzles, it provided

Hero of Alexandria demonstrates his aeolipile, *thought to be the world's first primitive steam engine. Hero tried to use the* aeolipile *to propel a vehicle, but the real breakthrough came much later.*

enough power to make the ball rotate. Hero tried to use the energy generated by his *aeolipile* to propel a vehicle.

But the first real breakthrough in using steam to propel a vehicle did not come until the 1600s. One of the scientists experimenting with steam at the time was a Jesuit priest named Ferdinand Verbiest. A native of Flanders, Father Verbiest went to China in 1659 to serve as a missionary. It did not take him long to impress the Chinese emperor with his scientific learning. During the early 1670s, probably as one of his mechanical experiments, Father Verbiest built for the emperor a steam-powered vehicle.

Father Verbiest's creation may have been the very first truly self-propelled vehicle. A small-scale cart driven by a steam engine, or turbine, it had a light body and was designed to be used indoors. No one is sure whether it was meant to carry passengers. The chassis, the part of a vehicle that usually holds the body and motor, was a wooden platform with four wheels. Bracketed above the chassis, about halfway between the front and rear wheels, was a large vessel called the *Aeolus-Kugel*. It held water heated by a container in which coal burned. The steam generated by the hot water provided the power to propel the cart. The cart could run for about an hour before the water vessel had to be filled again.

The Importance of the Engine

Not all those working to harness steam cared about—or even thought of—using it to propel a vehicle. In 1698, for example, an English engineer named Thomas Savery created a crude steam engine. It was not much like the engine of today and was far from efficient. But it was the first machine to provide mechanical power by harnessing steam.

About seven years later, another Englishman, an ironmonger named Thomas Newcomen, created a new kind of steam engine, an "atmospheric engine." Like Savery's engine, this one was stationary. It had a vertical container shaped like a can and called a cylinder. Inside it was a rod called a piston. As steam was produced and then condensed, it heated and then cooled the cylinder. Although not very fast or efficient, Newcomen's engine improved on Savery's and was less dangerous.

Then a Scots instrument maker named James Watt came along. While he was working at the University of

James Watt successfully redesigned the steam engine. His engines did not propel vehicles but did inspire other inventors whose work led in this direction.

Glasgow in Scotland, Watt was asked to repair one of Newcomen's engines. Watt not only repaired it, he came up with some features to improve it. The result was a new type of engine, which Watt patented in 1769.

Seven years later, Watt offered his engines for sale. Like most of the early engines, they could be used to power a cotton loom in a mill or to run a pump in a mine. Also like the others, they were too big and clumsy to use to propel a land vehicle. Still, they contributed to the development of the automobile because they gave other inventors, scientists, and engineers something to build

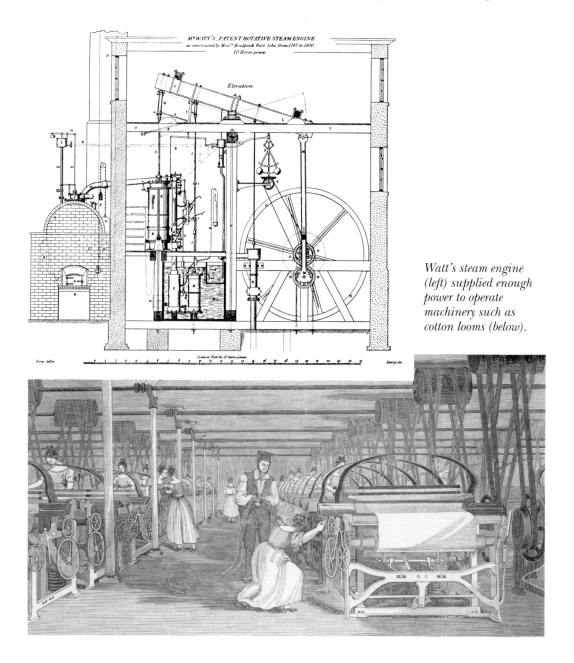

Watt's steam engine (left) supplied enough power to operate machinery such as cotton looms (below).

A Watt engine on display in a London museum. Watt's engines generated enough power for running looms and pumps but were too big and clumsy for powering land vehicles.

on and inspired them to create steam engines that could be used to make a self-moving vehicle.

The French Take the Lead

The real forerunner of all automobiles appeared in France in 1769, the same year in which Watt patented his steam engine in England. The French king, Louis XV, wanted a self-propelled vehicle that could tow heavy cannons for the army. So he instructed Captain Nicholas Joseph Cugnot, an engineer in the French artillery, to design something to do the job.

Cugnot, tired of depending on horses to pull heavy artillery, did as he was ordered. First, he designed an engine in which high-pressure steam was forced directly against each of two pistons. Then he designed a road vehicle to be propelled by the engine. In 1769, with the authorization of the minister of war, Cugnot built the first full-scale, steam-propelled road vehicle—a monstrous three-wheeled tractor. Mounted on the floor was a bench seat for a driver and three passengers. Hanging over the front wheel was a huge copper kettle that held water. The water was heated by a coal fire. The steam raised by the fire entered two cylinders and turned the heavy front wheel by rods.

Cugnot's bulky machine could not travel very fast—about 2 or 2.5 miles an hour. And it had to keep stopping to build up steam; it ran out of steam every 10 minutes or so. As a result, no cannon was ever mounted on it. All the same, these early efforts were enough to convince the military that Cugnot should be allowed to continue his work.

Sponsored by the French minister of war, Cugnot spent the next year or so reworking his design and building another vehicle. This one was more powerful, could haul a 4-ton gun, and could travel up to 3 or 4 miles per hour. Three-wheeled like the earlier model, it too had a large copper boiler and an engine with two cylinders that hung out beyond the front wheel. But it was

Nicholas Joseph Cugnot's monstrous three-wheeled steam carriage belched smoke and fire and made a lot of noise, yet it is considered the forerunner of the modern car.

heavy and badly balanced. It also was hard to maneuver and had to stop often for water.

Noisy, belching smoke and fire, the massive steam wagon began to inch its way along the road that ran from Paris to the city of Vincennes. Cugnot sat tall in the driver's seat. But, after he had gone about 3 miles, he had what was probably the world's first "automobile" accident. Taking a sharp turn at top speed, he ran into a wall and overturned the vehicle. This was easy to do because when the front wheel was turned—for example, to change direction—the kettle and engine turned with it. Thus the machine's center of gravity shifted, and the resulting imbalance led to disaster.

Cugnot was arrested, and the police took charge of his steam wagon. The project was abandoned, and the vehicle was never again driven on public streets. But the dream did not die. Cugnot had changed the basic function of the wheel. Until now, wheels had served to reduce the friction between a load and the surface of the ground. Cugnot, however, had used his engine to send power to the wheels themselves, making the wheels the levers that actually drove the load. Cugnot's steam wagon, the first horseless carriage, became the direct ancestor of the automobile and thus of all self-propelled vehicles.

The Triumph of Oliver Evans

For the next few decades, creative inventors and designers in different parts of the world built other experimental steam vehicles. The first vehicle ever that could run on both land and water was built in America. This was a truly special feat, considering world events of the time.

In 1776, when James Watt first offered his engines for sale, the American colonies were at war with England. By the time the war was over, Watt was making new engines that were better than his earlier ones. Americans, however, still could not benefit from Watt's experience because in 1785 the British Parliament made all export sales illegal. Most of the Americans trying to help modernize their country through the use of steam had never even seen a steam engine.

It was under these circumstances that Oliver Evans, a young inventor from the Crown Colony of Delaware, came to be known as "the American Watt" and the person responsible for the beginning of the American automobile. Evans had invented a steam engine. As early as 1773, he had talked to people about using his invention to "propel carriages."

Evans had gotten the idea for a steam-propelled land carriage in 1772 after hearing a story about an informal experiment conducted by a blacksmith's son. The boy had stopped up the opening of a rifle through which the powder was ignited. Then he had filled the rifle's long barrel with water and stuffed the end of the barrel tightly with cloth. Next he had put the part of the rifle to the rear of the barrel into the fire his father was using. Soon the water turned to steam, there was a loud cracking sound, and the wad of cotton shot out with great force. The rifle had produced a shot, just as if it had been loaded with gunpowder. Evans later wrote that upon hearing the story, "It immediately occurred to me that there was a power capable of propelling any wagon, provided that I could apply it, and I set myself to work to find out the means of doing so."

For a long time, Evans's efforts were frustrated. He could not get the tools, materials, and skilled labor he needed in the colonies. When the revolutionary war began in 1775 Evans set aside his inventing to serve in the Continental

Oliver Evans's 1801 steam engine. The small illustration in the upper right hand corner shows the engine being used to run a road vehicle.

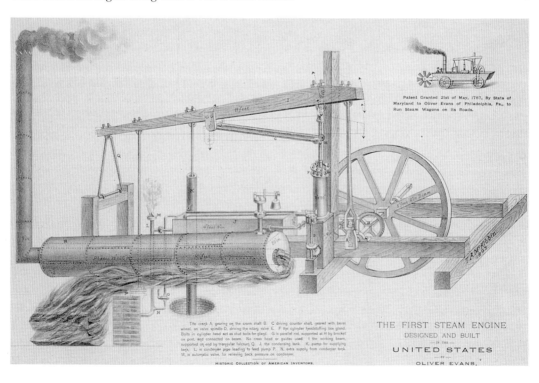

Evans believed demand for his Orukter Amphibolos *would grow once people saw how well his vehicle performed. This did not happen, much to his dismay.*

army. It was 1787 before Evans could convince the State of Maryland to give him and him alone the right to develop his steam wagon.

Evans was 50 years old when he finally got a chance to demonstrate that his small, high-pressure steam engine could move great loads over the road. His chance came in 1805 when the Philadelphia Board of Health wanted a dredge (a machine to clear sediment from waterways) to deepen its docks. The city contracted with Evans, who agreed to build a steam-powered floating dredge that would do the job.

Evans built an entirely new engine for his dredge. This engine, which used steam under pressure, developed more power than the atmospheric engines designed by Newcomen and Watt. Evans called his vehicle *Orukter Amphibolos*,

"Amphibious Digger." When it was completed, it was huge—30 feet long and 12 feet wide—and weighed 20 tons. An account written at the time described it as "a steam engine, on board of a flat-bottomed boat, to work a chain of hooks to break up the ground with buckets to raise it above the water, and deposit it in another boat to be carried off."

Steam Power for Land and Sea

On July 13, 1805, in a Philadelphia newspaper, Evans announced a public demonstration of his marvelous new invention. He urged "every generous person" to donate 25 cents to see the vehicle perform. He wanted to prove to everyone that steam could move land vehicles as well as boats. At the same time, he intended to show that he could build large, self-propelled land vehicles that would carry larger loads in less time and for greater profit than horse-drawn wagons. He was sure that once people saw this for themselves, some of them would offer to finance the manufacture of his steam engines.

Evans had built his *Orukter* away from the water. To get it the mile and a half to the river, he put axles and wheels under it, ran a belt from the engine, and used steam power. Thus Evans became the first American to build and operate a self-propelled vehicle.

Once the massive vehicle was on the river, Evans sailed it to Philadelphia, where it was to be launched. Upon arriving in Philadelphia, he ran it up the riverbank onto the land. It was on exhibition for several days, circling the water works at Center Square at a rate of 3 or 4 miles an hour. Then it was put to work around the docks in the Schuylkill River. The city of Philadelphia used it for the next three summers and then scrapped it.

Evans did not get the response he had expected, and the *Orukter* was the only steam wagon he ever built. He died in 1819 in New York City and was buried there in a grave bearing no memorial. Early on, he had made this prediction: "The time will come when people will travel by steam engines, from one city to another, almost as fast as birds fly. A carriage will set out from Washington in the morning, the passengers will breakfast at Baltimore, dine in Philadelphia, and sup in New York the same day." It sounded crazy at the time, but not many years were to pass before the prediction came true.

The British Contribute: Trevithick's Experiment

At about the same time Oliver Evans was experimenting in America, inventors in Great Britain were performing their own experiments. Among these was a mining engineer from Cornwall,

A reproduction of Evans's vehicle, Orukter Amphibolos. *Evans wanted to prove that a steam engine could propel a vehicle on land and in the water.*

named Richard Trevithick, who came to be known as the creator of locomotive power.

In 1800 Trevithick invented a high-pressure steam engine. On Christmas Eve of the following year, in London, he showed what the engine could do. He had designed a horseless carriage that would run on the power generated by the engine. The carriage had a horizontal boiler that produced the steamy clouds of wood smoke that drove its huge wood and metal rear wheels. The wheels, in fact, were much larger than the body of the passenger coach. The driver, whose job was to steer the small front wheels, sat in front. With its tall chimney stack and footplate for the man who would stoke the fire, Trevithick's horseless carriage looked more like a railway locomotive than like a car.

Richard Trevithick's self-propelled carriage could move uphill, according to one passenger, "faster than a man could walk."

The friends Trevithick took along for the ride that Christmas Eve became the first passengers transported by steam power. According to one of them, "When we see'd that Captain Dick was agoing to turn on steam, we jumped up, as many as could, maybe seven or eight of us. 'Twas a stiffish hill, but she went off like a bird." The writer went on to marvel that Trevithick had driven his coach "up that hill faster than a man could walk."

Trevithick had produced a self-propelled carriage that could travel at a speed of nearly 10 miles per hour. This was the first practical use of mechanical power to move a vehicle; Trevithick had built the first successful road engine.

Unfortunately, on another demonstration run four days later, Trevithick's creation broke down. Leaving the contraption in a stable, he and his cousin headed for a nearby hotel for "a roast goose and proper drinks." But they forgot to put out the fire that heated the carriage's boiler. Before long, the water boiled away and the vehicle caught fire. Both the vehicle and the stable burned up.

A Second Try

Undaunted, Trevithick persuaded his cousin to help him build a new, improved vehicle in which the steam could be raised more rapidly and kept going longer. The wheels on the new vehicle were 10 feet in diameter. This raised the coach so high that its passengers sat 6 feet above the ground.

Trevithick and his cousin drove the noisy, bouncing carriage along the bumpy streets of London, scaring people and horses alike. Trevithick had hoped

Trevithick's steam carriage, with its huge rear wheels, small front wheel, and its hissing, smoking steam engine, was a sight to behold on London streets in the early 1800s.

the demonstrations would convince someone to sponsor him. But this did not happen. Frustrated and very disappointed, he ended up taking the vehicle apart. After selling the engine to a mill owner who wanted to use it to power his mill, Trevithick set about building a locomotive for a railroad company.

The work of Trevithick and Evans was to have a major impact on both road and railway transportation. When Evans made his prediction that "one day people would travel by steam engines almost as fast as birds fly," little did he know that steam engines were only the beginning.

CHAPTER 2

The Infant Years

By the early 1800s, steam engines were being put to good use on the roadways in Europe, propelling passenger carriages. The people of the time did not know it, but these vehicles represented a major step toward the concept of the automobile. The emergence of that concept between 1880 and 1890, however, was due in great part to the self-propelled steam coach and the bicycle.

Road Locomotives and Bicycles

The earliest steam carriages made their greatest impact in England, where they were known as steam coaches or "road

The London and Birmingham steam coach had open-air seating for 22 passengers and inside seating for 28.

locomotives." England had been at war with France. After the war, in the early 1800s, commerce began to develop fast, both at home and overseas. British roads, though, were not very good—often just dirt paths or country lanes. This made long-distance traveling a hardship for many merchants. The merchants complained and their complaints led to the development of new, simpler, and cheaper ways to build roads. With new and better roads, creative engineers began to develop self-propelled steam coaches to travel along them.

By the 1820s, British companies were being formed to operate steam-powered passenger coaches, and a few ambitious men set up networks of passenger routes for their vehicles. One of these entrepreneurs was a chemist from Cornwall, Sir Goldsworthy Gurney. The passenger coaches, or steam diligences, in his network carried 21 people, who were more than pleased that they could travel 14 miles in just an hour's time. Another innovator was Walter Hancock, who was only 25 years old in 1824 when he designed and built his first steamer. By 1831, he had started a regular bus service—one steam-propelled carriage called *Infant*—that carried delighted passengers between two towns. Within three years, Hancock had at least nine carriages in operation. New businesses and industries were needed to service the carriages. Hancock helped to fill this need by setting up a chain of service stations and garages in London.

As pleased as some people were with steam coaches, to others they were anything but wonderful. Farmers thought they were noisy and smelly and protested that they frightened horses and other animals. People who owned some of the roads did not like the carriages either. The coaches, they said, tore up the roads. So they charged steam coach companies a lot more than they charged horse coach companies to use them. Stagecoach and railroad operators did not like the steam coaches either because they were competition, and competition could mean less profit. Other people simply did not think the steam coaches were necessary. Why, they asked, do we need these "cumbersome contrivances" when the railroads are doing a perfectly fine job of carrying goods and passengers?

As a result of these and other pressures, the British government began to regulate the use of the self-propelled vehicles. A strict law passed in 1865 was called the Red Flag Act because it ordered that when a self-propelled steam vehicle was on the road, a person carrying a red flag had to walk ahead of it to warn people that it was coming. That was during the daytime. At night, someone had to walk in front carrying a lantern. The act also imposed a speed limit on the vehicles—4 miles per hour on open ground and 2 miles per hour in towns. This meant that most passengers could get where they were going as fast or faster by foot.

Although the Red Flag Act and other laws worked to slow the development of motoring for years, the bicycle helped to speed up the introduction of the automobile. Because of bicycles, engineers learned a lot about how to design and produce structures that did not weigh a great deal but were strong. Not only could bicycle owners go places easier and faster than on foot, but they did not need the railroad to travel; they could—and did—do it on their own. Then too, as the number of bicycle owners grew, so did interest in building new and better roads. One

An 1896 poster touts the benefits of bicycling. Inspired by the bicycle, engineers worked to create a strong, lightweight, self-propelled vehicle.

American automobile maker explained it this way:

> The bicycle created a new demand which it was beyond the ability of the railroad to supply. Then it came about that the bicycle could not satisfy the demand which it had created. A mechanically propelled vehicle was wanted instead of a foot-propelled one, and we know now that the automobile was the answer.

The automaker was right. Beginning about 1880, light three- and four-wheeled automobiles based on the bicycle began to appear, most of them powered by steam or by electricity.

Serpollet's Flash Boiler

In France, meanwhile, engineers and others experimented with steam and built self-propelled vehicles. Around 1875, an exciting breakthrough was made by Léon Serpollet, the 17-year-old son of a blacksmith. The steam-powered vehicles that had appeared to this point had to have a heavy water tank, or boiler, to store a supply of steam. Serpollet came up with a new kind of boiler called a flash boiler. In Serpollet's boiler, water was pumped into a heated metal tube bent into coils and was converted right away into superheated steam. This meant that steam was generated only as it was needed in the engine. Since the boiler never built up a heavy concentration of steam, people no longer had to worry about explosions.

Before long Serpollet took out a patent for a car that used his flash boiler. The vehicle had three wheels and a single seat, and the driver had to use the handlebar to steer it. But it could go as fast as 7 miles an hour and could travel 12 miles before the driver had to refill the water tank under the seat. Getting the car started took a little time. First, the driver had to light a charcoal fire in the firebox mounted next to the boiler behind the rear axle. Then, for the next 10 minutes or so, he had to wait for the tube to heat. When

Léon Serpollet's three-wheeled vehicle attracted lots of attention, including from police who worried that it might be a hazard on city streets.

The Stanley brothers take a drive in their first steam car, the Stanley Steamer.

the tube was hot enough, he could work the lever that pumped the water into the tube. At this point, a pump driven by an engine under the seat took over, and the car got under way.

Not everyone was as sure as Serpollet that the car was not a hazard to others. For a while, the inventor had to get special permission from the police each time he wanted to take the car on the road. In time, though, the police gave him a permanent permit to drive his vehicle. By 1900, Serpollet had a fair number of customers for his car, including the Prince of Wales.

The Stanley Steamer

Road networks like those found in Europe did not exist in the United States in the early and middle 1800s. So passenger carriages and "buses"—early mass transportation—did not develop as they had abroad. But that did not keep Americans from experimenting with self-propelled vehicles. In fact, it did not take the Americans long to overtake the Europeans and make the steam car their own. France led the world in the design of steam cars in the late 1800s and early 1900s. But most of the more than 100 makes on the market were made by Americans.

Of all the manufacturers of steam-driven automobiles, the most well-known were twin brothers, Francis E. (F.E.) and Freeland O. (F.O.) Stanley. Born on a farm in Maine, the Stanley brothers were identical in almost every way. Their father, a farmer and part-time school teacher, wanted the twins to become school teachers. At first, F.O. did just that. But F.E. bought a photographer's shop in Maine, the first of three. In 1883 F.E. made a major tech-

Because the Stanley Steamer looked so much like a horse-drawn buggy, it was referred to as the "horseless buggy."

nical breakthrough in photography and, before long, the brothers were running their own successful photographic plate business in Newton, Massachusetts, near Boston. One day in 1896 the brothers went to a fair in a nearby town. One of the attractions was the promised track performance of a steam car imported from Europe. Upon seeing the car break down before it had completed a single lap, F.E. determined that he could build a better one. "Well, boys," he promised, "before another fall passes I will show you a self-propelled carriage that will go around that track not only once but several times without stopping!"

F.E. made good his promise. In October of 1897, the twins produced the original Stanley Steamer—a two-seater on spoked wheels like those of a bicycle, with a boiler and a two-cylinder steam engine in a box that served as the driver's seat. That Steamer was just the beginning for the Stanleys. From the beginning, F.E. and F.O. worked to improve their cars. They showed them off at meets and auto competitions, and the orders came pouring in. Between the fall of 1898 and the fall of 1899, they built 200 Steamers and sold every one of them. All were small two-seaters with an engine and a boiler under the seats. The boiler was shaped like a drum and held about 300 vertical tubes surrounded by water. Below was a burner that sent heated gas up the tubes and eventually out a smokebox at the back of the car. The Stanley brothers had good reason to be proud of their steamer. The car performed amazingly well for the time—traveling up to 25 miles an hour and going about 60 miles before running out of fuel and water.

By 1903, the Stanleys had 140 people working for them and were producing and selling three cars a day. In their best years, they produced and sold from 650 to 1,000 cars a year. For many years, the Stanleys did not advertise their cars, and they always did business strictly on their own terms. A person who wanted to buy a Steamer had to write the brothers. If they thought the buyer deserved the car, they wrote back, indicating when to pick it up. Buyers paid cash—$750 in 1903. Cars came in one color—black. Dissatisfied buyers could return their cars and get their money back.

The Steamers looked so much like the traditional horse-drawn buggy that people began to call them "horseless buggies." The engine of the Stanley Steamer was light enough for a strong man to pick up with one hand. There were only 13 interior parts—no starter, no clutch, no gears. The car could go forward or backward. A lever on the steering column controlled the speed, which in passenger models went as high as 60 miles per hour. Since early models could go only about a mile on a gallon of water, drivers often stopped at horse troughs to refill. In Vermont, this led a disgruntled legislator to push for a law that barred "these snorting demons from facilities set out for the comfort and well-being of a man's noble friend and helper, the horse."

The concept behind the steam car was simple. It burned gasoline or kerosene as a fuel to boil water held in a tank. From the boiling water came steam. The pressure of the steam that

In the mid-nineteenth century, fire departments began trading in their horse-drawn carriages for steam engines such as this 1858 model.

escaped from the tank set in motion the driving mechanism. This meant that before a steam car could move, it had to "get up a head of steam." For the driver of a Stanley, steaming up and getting under way took about 20 minutes.

The process went something like this. Step 1: Work a lever on the floor to build up fuel pressure. Step 2: Take a piece of hose connected to a small acetylene tank in the tool kit, open a valve on the tank, and light a nozzle on the end of the hose. Step 3: Hold the flame over the pilot jet to get it hot. Step 4: Open the pilot valve. Step 5: Light the pilot light. Step 6: Open the firing-up valve and let the kerosene or gasoline warm up by burning on the main burner for about 30 seconds. Step 7: Open the valve to the main fuel tank and wait for the paraffin to begin to heat the water in the boiler under the hood. For the car to start, the flames must be roaring and the steam pressure gauge must read around 300. Step 8: Release the hand brake so the wheels can turn.

The last Stanley model was made in 1925, but there was little interest in it.

Other steamers—Olds, Whites, Dobles, Locomobiles—had stopped production or were on the verge of doing so. Steam cars had improved greatly over the years. They could go farther on a tankful of water because a condenser had been developed that allowed boiled water to be recycled. They were less dangerous because the open-flame pilot light under the boiler had been replaced by a unit that was lit electrically. They even became easier to start. The 1923 Doble could be started up by turning a key on the car's dashboard, or front panel. But, even with these and other improvements, the day of the steamer was soon over.

A Different Kind of Horseless Carriage

At the same time the steamer was capturing the imagination of some people, electric cars were catching the interest of others. The first crude electric car was built in 1839 by a Scot named Robert Anderson. In 1869 a French-

The first crude electric car was built in 1839. By the turn of the century, the electric car was a popular mode of transportation for wealthy Americans and Europeans.

Though the electric car was easy to start and operate, nonpolluting, and long-lasting, its popularity waned by the mid-1920s.

man—Gaston Plante—took the next major step when he invented an accumulator, or storage battery. About 20 years later, in Boston, Fred Kimball produced the first battery-driven car in America. And in 1890 William Morrison of Des Moines, Iowa, became the first man to manufacture and sell an electric car. By 1900, electric cars were almost everywhere. Large fleets of electric cabs prowled the streets of London and Paris, and the first taxis—electrics with batteries that weighed about a ton—appeared on the streets of New York. Electric cars, however, were for the rich. In England, they were viewed as a gentleman's carriage and were driven by uniformed chauffeurs. In America, where they were limited to city use, they became especially popular with women because they were easy to operate.

The design of the electric car was simple. Under the hood were storage batteries, which heavy cables connected to a powerful motor mounted in front of the rear axle. The electric car had several advantages over the steam car.

For one, the engine started immediately. For another, the electric ran almost silently and smoothly and did not vibrate. It did not pollute the air with smelly fumes. And, it was easy to operate and to control, with hardly any moving parts that would wear out.

The electrics, however, did have some drawbacks. The greatest was that they could not carry an adequate power source. The batteries were bulky, heavy, and expensive. They were not reliable and had to be recharged every 20 to 40 miles, which also was expensive. The annual maintenance costs could run as high as the original purchase price. Another drawback was that most electric cars could not travel very fast—30 miles an hour at best. In 1900 most ambled along at about 12 miles per hour.

In the late 1890s and early 1900s, the electrics were not as popular as the steamers. But, for some people, they were perfect. One gentleman of the time gave this advice to prospective car owners: "If you use your carriage simply for shopping or making calls or going

One disadvantage of the electric car was its battery that had to be recharged every 20 to 40 miles. Here, a wire runs from the car battery to its charging source.

for short drives, or for driving a short distance to business every day, *and for nothing else*, then I advise you to buy an electromobile, which of all town carriages is the most luxurious and convenient. But for any other purpose the electric carriage is the least useful and most expensive form of motor-car."

Electric cars did not stay popular very long. By 1910, they had all but vanished from the streets of London and Paris. The electric automobiles had been the most popular in America. But even there they soon lost popularity. One American company offered an electric model on special order until the late 1930s, but most of the 20 or so different American manufacturers had stopped marketing electrics by the mid-1920s.

CHAPTER 3

The New Kid on the Road

The popularity of electric and steam cars did not last very long for many reasons, but the biggest reason was the development of a third kind of car. This car looked almost exactly like a steam car and could travel at about the same speeds. But it started up much faster, and there were no blazing flames, pilot lights, or hissing steam to worry about. This car got its power from a different kind of engine, one that inventors in France, England, and Germany had been developing since 1860. Known as the internal combustion engine, it is still used in most cars today.

The Internal Combustion Engine

The first internal combustion engine was patented in Paris in 1860, just three years after gasoline was developed. That year, a Belgian named Jean Joseph Etienne Lenoir registered his new invention—an engine that worked by burning coal gas inside a cylinder that also contained air and a piston. When an electric spark lit the gas and air, tiny explosions, or combustions, erupted inside the cylinder. These "internals combustions" made the piston move up and down. Then, the up-and-down movement induced a rotary, or spinning, movement by a heavy metal wheel called a flywheel. When this movement was carried by belts and chains to machine parts, the parts themselves began

to move. This new engine of Lenoir's was based on steam engines. But it was different from them because it used internal combustions to move the piston.

On a summer day in 1862, in a forest near Paris, Lenoir proved that his engine could propel a vehicle. He took an old horse cart and mounted his engine between its wheels. Within a few minutes, the cart was bouncing slowly along, propelled by the sputtering engine. The cart did not go very fast or very far, and it used a lot of gas. Lenoir was not really satisfied with it. So he tinkered with it for a while longer. But soon he lost interest and turned his attention to other things.

Other people, however, took up the challenge. One of these was a German manufacturer, Nicolaus August Otto. A former traveling grocery salesman, Otto had no real technical background. But that did not stop him from experimenting with Lenoir's engine. He was sure he could improve it. At an exposition in Paris in 1867, Otto introduced his first version of an improved engine. It weighed 4,000 pounds, measured more than 15 feet long, and had to be supported by a concrete foundation. This engine would never be used to propel a road vehicle! Finally, in 1876, Otto patented and built a more practical and compact internal combustion engine called the Silent Otto. It was much faster and more efficient than Lenoir's engine. Lenoir's engine was a two-stroke engine: that is, for each explosion, the piston moved up and down two times. The Silent Otto, however, was a four-stroke engine: explosions in it were bigger, and each one caused the piston to go up and down four times. By 1900, Otto had sold thousands of his engines in Europe and the United States. Soon it was the most popular gasoline engine in the world, the one that became the model for the modern automobile engine.

Daimler and Benz

Otto did not develop his engine all by himself. He had help from an engineer named Gottlieb Daimler, who managed his factory. In 1882 Daimler and Otto had a falling out and Daimler resigned. He then set up an office and workshop with Wilhelm Maybach, a young designer who also had worked for Otto. The next year, Daimler built an engine

Nicolaus August Otto (above) created a successful gasoline engine called the Silent Otto (left) that became the model for the modern automobile engine.

THE FOUR-STROKE CYCLE

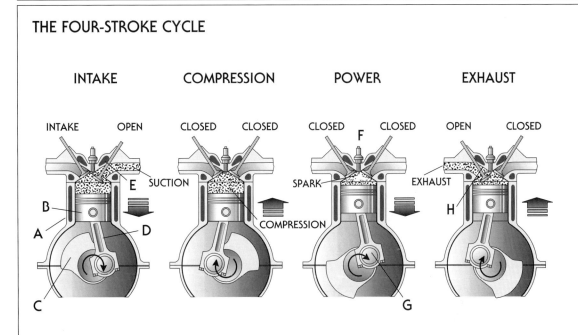

INTAKE	COMPRESSION	POWER	EXHAUST

The gasoline engine developed by Nicolaus August Otto in 1876 was the most powerful and efficient gasoline engine of its time. It derived its power from the controlled burning of fuel and air vapors inside a metal cylinder (A) that drove a piston (B) up and down in rapid, four-part motion. This motion became known as the four-stroke cycle. Piston-driven engines today still use the four-stroke cycle, which consists of:

Intake As the cam (C) rotates in a clockwise direction, it exerts downward pressure on the base of the connecting rod (D), which pulls the piston down the cylinder. The downward motion of the piston causes the cylinder to suck a mixture of fuel and air vapors through the intake valve (E). When the piston reaches the bottom of the cylinder, the intake valve closes, trapping the mixture of fuel and air vapors inside the cylinder.

Compression Continuing in a clockwise motion, the cam pushes the rod and the piston upward. The rising piston forces together, or compresses, the molecules of air and fuel inside the cylinder. As the mixture of fuel and air vapors compresses, it heats up, making it more volatile, or explosive.

Power When the piston reaches the top of the compression stroke, the spark plug (F) fires, causing an electric spark to jump across a small gap at the bottom of the spark plug. The spark ignites the fuel and air vapors, causing them to burn inside the cylinder. The burning vapors expand rapidly, driving the piston and rod downward and turning the cam. The cam turns the crankshaft (G), which in turn powers the wheels of the vehicle.

Exhaust Momentum from the power stroke keeps the cam turning, pushing the rod and piston upward once more. At the same time, the exhaust valve (H) opens. The head of the piston pushes the burned vapors up and out of the cylinder, past the exhaust valve. When the piston reaches the top of the stroke, the exhaust valve closes, the intake valve opens, and the four-stroke cycle begins again.

that weighed much less and worked faster and better than other engines. Because of a part called a carburetor, which Daimler had created in his design, the engine could run on liquid gasoline instead of coal gas or some other kind of gas. In 1885 Daimler fit his engine onto a two-wheel bicycle. In the dark of night, his 17-year-old son took it out on a test run, about 4 miles up the road and back and across a frozen lake. Daimler had "invented" the motorcycle.

Now that Daimler had added power to a bicycle, he wanted to do the same to a coach. A motorized four-wheeled vehicle, he thought, would make a perfect birthday gift for his wife. So, in early 1886, he placed an order with a lo-

A 1918 advertisement promotes the Daimler. Gottlieb Daimler's cars were among the first to be powered by high-speed internal combustion engines.

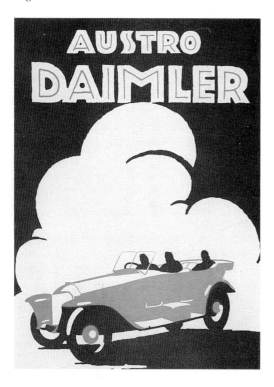

cal carriage builder for a "handsomely but solidly built coach" designed, of course, to be pulled by a horse. The coach was late in arriving, so an impatient Daimler put his engine in a boat instead—creating the first motorboat. When the coach finally arrived months later, Daimler set about adapting it— pulling off the shafts, installing steering gear, putting his engine between the front and back seats. In the end, Daimler created one of the first automobiles powered by a high-speed internal combustion engine. In 1890 he started a company to produce his cars—the Daimler Motor Company.

Less than 75 miles away from Daimler was the workshop of another German who had been working with engines—Karl Benz. When Benz was only 13 years old, he had seen a model of a steam engine in his science class. Then and there, he had determined that one day he would build a vehicle to run without rails. In 1871 Benz opened a workshop to make machine parts. The business failed, and he next turned his efforts to designing an engine for a road vehicle. On New Year's Eve, 1879, his first engine ran for the first time.

In the spring of 1885, Benz tested an engine of his own design on a machine with two large back wheels and a smaller front wheel steered by a tiller. He had wanted his car to have four wheels, but he had had doubts about how to design steering for a four-wheeled vehicle. Later that year, a triumphant Benz got a patent for a "carriage with gas engine." Benz, who had never seen a car before he built one himself, had created the first practical automobile powered by an internal combustion engine. It was not a very sturdy automobile. Its chassis was a steel

Karl Benz, who built his first automobile without ever having seen one, designed automobiles that outperformed all the others. Promotional posters tout the Benz automobile and engine.

tube frame. The engine, which was tucked under the driver's seat, had only one cylinder and the power of about three horses. But it was an improvement over Otto's engine, and some of the elements of the car were incorporated in later, more modern automobiles. The public did not find out about the car until the next year. One local newspaper made this prediction:

> The difficult task of inventing may now be considered at an end and Benz intends to proceed with the making of these vehicles for practical use. This motor vehicle is not meant to have the same purpose and characteristics as a velocipede [a bicycle or tricycle], which

one could take for a pleasurable spin over a smooth, well-kept country road; rather it is conceived as a cart or peasant's wagon, suitable not only for traveling fairly good roads but also for carrying heavy loads up steep inclines. For example, it would enable a commercial traveler to take his samples from one place to another without difficulty.

> We believe the wagon has a good future. When the speed is made sufficient it will be the cheapest promotional tool for traveling salesmen as well as a means for tourists to get around.

For the next several years, Benz and Daimler independently kept on working to improve engines and to make better vehicles to put them in. In 1900 Daimler died—without ever having met Benz. Karl Benz, though, lived long enough to see his company and Daimler's become one in 1926.

The Duryea Brothers

In the 1890s an article about a Benz automobile in *Scientific American* magazine caught the eye of two brothers, bicycle mechanics from Illinois—Charles E. and J. Frank Duryea. They were determined to produce their own gasoline-powered automobile. In 1893 they achieved their goal by attaching a one-cylinder internal combustion engine to the back of a much-used, high-wheeled horse buggy. They called their car a "buggynaut." It was America's first internal combustion car.

For the next two years, the Duryea brothers concentrated on designing and building a second, better model of automobile. On Thanksgiving Day, 1895, Frank drove a new, improved version in an auto race in Chicago. Europe

had already had its first real auto race. But this one, sponsored by the *Chicago Times-Herald* newspaper, was the first such competition held in the United States. Whoever won the race would take home a prize of $2,000—a lot of money for that time. Eighty cars entered the race, but only six made it to the starting line: two American electrics, three foreign entries—two of them Benz cars—and the Duryea, with Frank at the wheel. The race was supposed to have run about 80 miles. But the weather had turned bad the night before, so the race was shortened to a little over 50 miles. The roads, which had not been smooth to start with, were crusted with snow and ice. Nine hours after the start of the race, the first car slid across the finish line. It was the Duryea! Only one other car—a Benz—finished the race. The Duryea brothers used their prize money to start their own automobile manufacturing company, the Duryea Motor Wagon Company. The next year they produced and sold 13 cars, all the same design.

In 1897 the Duryeas pitted one of their autos against European cars and

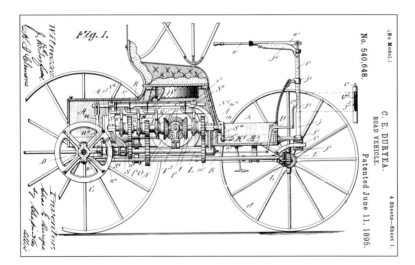

The Duryea brothers designed America's first internal combustion car. A patent diagram shows details of the Duryeas' car and engine design.

Car clubs and auto races drew many car enthusiasts, especially in Europe and America, where fondness for cars was growing.

drivers in a race in England. To the surprise of almost everyone, they came in ahead of many of the best Europeans. This performance won the rapidly growing American auto industry much publicity in Europe. Americans were already intrigued with the gasoline-powered car. The Duryeas' great showing in the race inspired many amateur inventors in the United States. If the Duryeas could design and build a vehicle that could beat the Europeans, so could they!

The Far from Perfect Automobile

By the mid-1890s, two New York companies, the Gimbel Brothers and R.H. Macy Company, were offering shoppers the chance to buy gasoline-powered horseless carriages. By the late 1890s, auto clubs had been founded in Europe and in the United States. Auto races, a testing ground for new ideas and a major source of publicity, were drawing greater numbers of entries and bigger crowds.

By then, imaginative engineers and designers had come up with ways to improve cars and to make them look less like horse carriages. The French had been especially busy. In fact, by the early 1900s, a model of French car called a roadster was the most popular car in Europe. Much of the change had come from two Frenchmen in particular—Emile Constant Levassor and René Panhard, who in 1891 did something no one else had done before. They put

Flat tires were a common frustration for early motorists. Poor roads and poorly made tires contributed to the problem.

the engine of their car up front under a covering called a hood, instead of in the rear or under the seat. They called their design the *système Panhard.* The vehicle actually looked like a car instead of like a tricycle, carriage, or buggy. With the new *système,* larger and more powerful engines could be used. A few years later, the French company came out with another first—an enclosed vehicle called a sedan.

Even with the improvements, a ride in an automobile was quite an adventure. Most of the early cars had no tops and no windshields, so there was nothing to keep out dust, dirt, rain, flying in-sects, or anything else that might be in the air. Mudguards around the wheels could go only so far in protecting mo-torists from the thick clouds of dust and dirt thrown up from the roads. The cars did not have heaters either, so only the bravest chose to ride in them once the weather turned cold. A lot of things could go wrong with these early cars. They broke down so much that one newspaper suggested that motorists take a pair of horses just in case.

The motorist who did not know how to fix a car was in trouble because there were no real repair shops and no walk-in outlets that sold replacement parts.

Tires were a big problem. They did next to nothing to cushion the bumps in the road, and they were always going flat. The early tires were fine for bicycles, but the weight of a car combined with the effects of bad roads wore them out very fast. Smart car owners carried special tire repair kits. Changing a tire was a dirty, time-consuming job. The tire had to come off the wheel, and the inner tube had to be pulled out. Then the motorist had to take a small patch of rubber from the repair kit, heat it, find the hole in the inner tube, and place the patch over it. Once the hole was patched, the inner tube could be put back in the tire and the tire pumped up and put back on the rim.

The cars were hard to start. It took muscle to get the engine going. Hanging from the front of the car was a long rod called a crank, which had to be turned until the flywheel attached to the pistons started spinning. Once the pistons started moving up and down, internal combustion would begin. Cranking the engine is what got it going, but there was always a danger that the engine would backfire while the crank was being turned, causing the crank to snap backward. Even though backfires could be avoided by adjusting a lever before starting to crank, more than one poor motorist got a broken arm from cranking the engine. Stopping was less work but just as hazardous. Brakes were connected to the rear wheels only and had to be operated by hand. More often than not, they did not work very well.

Two motorists stand by their disabled vehicle after an accident. Accidents occurred even with improvements such as the windshield, lights, and horns.

Before steering wheels were added to cars about 1900, motorists steered with a tiller, a vertical stick in the middle of the car, or tiller wheel, a small wheel attached to a vertical stick.

The cars were not easy to drive either, and many motorists had a hard time controlling them. Most cars were steered with a tiller or a small tiller wheel that sat atop an upright column in the middle of the car. There were no steering wheels until about 1900. There were, however, levers of all kinds, each with a different purpose. There were levers to make the car go faster or slower, to open the valves, to adjust the engine settings, and so on. The motorist had to know what each lever was for and how and when to use it. It was easy to get confused and use the wrong lever or to push the right lever backward instead of forward. The condition of the roads did not help. Accidents were about as common as breakdowns. Beginning in the very early 1900s, cars had to be registered, and owners were required to display a number plate in most countries, mainly because the authorities needed a way to identify and keep track of reckless drivers.

The cars were dangerous to the people and animals unlucky enough to get in their path. There were still numerous horseback riders and horse-drawn carriages and carts on the roads, especially in rural areas. Most of the horses were afraid of cars, and many reared and bolted at the sight of one. Some horses broke into a furious gallop, pulling a carriage and its panic-filled occupants behind them. Soon warning devices—horns, bells, gongs, and so on—were required. But these noisemakers scared the horses and stray animals more than they helped them.

Automobiles were noisy, troublesome, unsettling, and costly. But that did not stop them from making progress and growing more popular. Even people who spoke out against them had to admit that they had some advantages over the horse and the railroad. They were faster than horses and had more stamina, and they did not have to stop and rest the way horses did. Trains did not have to stop and rest either, but they ran on a set schedule and could go only where tracks had been laid. Often there was no train station close to the place a person wanted to go. This meant taking a train and then hiring a horse to finish the journey. With cars, people could go where they wanted when they wanted.

By 1900, the automobile was a fact of life both in Europe and in the United States. For Europeans, motor cars had come to be a sign of wealth and sophistication, and by the end of 1910 most upper-class Europeans owned one. So did most upper-class Americans. For Europeans, this was enough. But for some Americans, it was not. One such American was Henry Ford. "I'm going to democratize the automobile," he proclaimed. "When I'm through everyone will be able to afford one, and everyone will have one." When Ford did what he said he would, it changed society for all time.

CHAPTER 4

Growth of an Industry

It has been said that while others invent, Americans improve. This was not always true. But it was the case in the late 1800s and early 1900s when it came to the automobile. The gasoline automobile had first appeared in Germany. By about 1890, automotive production on a commercial scale had begun in France. The Americans did not start producing automobiles commercially for about another 8 or 10 years. But, when they did, they revolutionized the industry, improved the automobile, and made it a necessary part of life for the rich and the not-so-rich alike.

The Pioneering Spirit

In November 1900, the first auto show in America was held in New York City's Madison Square Garden. Excitement ran high. Automobile manufacturers—there were now about 30 in the nation—could show off their amazing machines, and anyone with enough money could actually buy a car at the show. Many Americans still had reservations about the new contraptions. As they saw it, automobiles were dangerous, expensive toys for the wealthy, meant to be driven on racetracks rather than roads. One farmers' group in Pennsylvania went so far as to tell its members to patrol the highways on Sundays, shoot at drivers of automobiles, and threaten to have them arrested. Even so, because of the gasoline engine, there were more

cars on the road, and manufacturers were trying to improve them and to make them safer.

American inventors had been tinkering with the idea of a horseless carriage for a great many years. In 1877 a New York patent attorney and amateur inventor named George Selden had designed and built a horseless carriage, complete with a two-cylinder internal combustion engine to propel it. But it was not until 1900 that some farsighted Americans began to look at the automobile not as a toy for the rich but as an exciting and marketable product, a good way to make money. Among these were men who gained fame as pioneers of the automobile industry, including David D. Buick, William C. Durant, Henry N. Leland, and Ransom E. Olds. All four lived in Michigan, and all played a major part in the development of the automobile. They and others like them helped to usher in the machine age in transportation.

David Dunbar Buick was the son of Scottish immigrants. Orphaned at age 5, he grew up to become the owner of a prosperous machine engine company. Buick was an inventor who counted among his creations a lawn sprinkler, an enameled bathtub, and some other devices that had to do with indoor toilets. In 1903 Buick built his first car. The next year, he sold his first car. By the end of 1904 he had produced 37 cars, which he sold for $850 each. By the end of the decade, Buick was one of the top

George Selden and his son pose with their gasoline-powered motor vehicle. The year of its invention, 1877, is painted on the side of the car.

10 carmakers in the nation. Much of this success was due to the efforts of a former carriage maker from Flint, Michigan, William C. Durant, who used his business and financial know-how to convert Buick's company into a money-making operation. In 1908 Durant brought together Buick and a number of other automobile companies to form a giant new automobile manufacturing company—General Motors.

One of the members of General Motors was the Cadillac Company. Named after Antoine de la Mothe Cadillac, the founder of Detroit, it had been started by a master mechanic and engine designer named Henry M. Leland. At the time, car parts were not turned out to exact, or precise, measurements. Instead, each part was made to fit with the other parts that went into a particular car. This meant that even though two cars were the same model, made by the same company, there was a good chance that their parts were not interchangeable. Leland thought that parts should be made so accurately that all items of the same kind would be exactly the same, no matter how many were made. "Even though you make thousands," he explained, "the first and last should be precisely alike." In 1908 Leland made a major breakthrough for the automobile industry—he produced the first automobiles with interchangeable parts. Four years later, Cadillac introduced another innovation for the automobile—an electric self-starter. This was a dream come true for motorists. Hand-cranking was hard work. The electric starter meant no more hand-cranking. As a result, more women began to want to drive a car.

Another major breakthrough had been made several years earlier—in

1901—by a machinist named Ransom Eli Olds. Olds had started out building steam cars. When he sold one to a merchant in Bombay, India, it became the first American car to be shipped overseas. In 1899 Olds had turned away from steam and had set up the Olds Motor Vehicle Company to manufacture gasoline-powered cars. Two years later, he built more than 400 two-cylinder, tiller-steered automobiles with curved dashboards. Not only was the curved dash new and different, but no other plant in the nation had ever produced so many gasoline-fueled cars in a single year!

Olds had been the first to put the automobile into large-scale or mass production. Until then, both in Europe and in America, building a car had been a slow, dull, time-consuming pro-

Ransom Eli Olds (above) started the Olds Motor Vehicle Company to manufacture gasoline-powered cars. At left, an 1897 tiller-steered Oldsmobile.

cess. The person who built it made each part, then put the parts together like the pieces of a jigsaw puzzle, fitting each with the next, one at a time, by hand. This method of building a car kept the number produced low and the prices high. Olds knew that in Europe the car was a luxury only for the rich. He thought that was fine for Europe but believed that there was a bigger, broader market in the United States. He wanted to produce cars faster, more cheaply, and in greater quantity. So, instead of making each part himself, he spelled out his requirements and contracted with some machine shops to make the parts for him. He used the time he would have spent making the parts to concentrate on ways to assemble them quickly without spending a lot of money. Olds did not "invent" mass production. It had been experimented with many years before in Europe and in the United States. He was, however, the first to use mass production techniques to make gasoline-powered automobiles.

Ford's Car for the Great Multitude

Michigan was the home of yet another automobile pioneer, the one some say "jacked up the world and slid four wheels under it." That man was Henry Ford. Ford's father was a farmer who had emigrated from Ireland. But farm life was not for young Henry. He preferred tinkering with machinery. When he was a teenager, he left the farm and went to Detroit, where he apprenticed to a machinist. In time, his mechanical skill got him a job as an engineer with a local electric company.

In his spare time, Ford began building engines and automobiles. On Christmas Eve, 1893, he and his wife Clara tested his first gasoline engine. The engine, with its cylinder made out of one-inch pipe and its homemade piston, was ignited by ordinary house current. With the engine perched over the kitchen sink, Clara slowly, carefully poured gasoline into the intake valve.

An artist depicts Henry Ford, one of the pioneers of automobile manufacturing, pushing his first car from the shed that served as his shop.

A replica of the brick shed where Ford built his first car, a two-speed with tiller-steering and a top speed of 25 miles per hour.

To their delight, the engine actually fired up and ran.

Three years later, based on plans he had seen in an article in *American Machinist* magazine, Ford built another engine and his first automobile. The car had a tiller to steer it, four bicycle wheels, and two speeds. It did not have a reverse gear, or a brake. Ford had built the car inside a brick shed behind his house. When it turned out that the car was wider than the shed door, Ford had to knock down part of the wall with an axe to get the car out for a test run. The car ran fine, but it was noisy enough to be branded a public nuisance.

Ford built other cars after that and started several businesses to manufacture them. But the businesses failed. Far from ready to give up, he set out to produce a bigger, more powerful, much faster car and to get lots of publicity for it. He built the car. Then he hired a top-notch bicycle rider named Barney Oldfield to drive it in a race. Oldfield won the race, the car got the publicity Ford wanted, and Ford got the backing he needed to open the Ford Motor Company in 1903. The way to make automobiles, he decided, is "to make one automobile like another automobile, to make them all alike." He immediately produced the $850 Model A, "the boss of the road." According to Ford Company advertisements, it was "positively the most perfect machine on the market, having overcome all drawbacks such as smell, noise, jolt, etc. common to all other makes of Auto Carriages. It is so simple that a boy of 15 can run it."

The next year, Ford came out with a bigger, more expensive car. Two years after that, he introduced an even bigger, heavier, and more costly model.

When it did not sell well, Ford decided to change his tactics and to forget about the big, expensive cars everyone else was producing. Instead, he would build "the universal automobile," "a motor car for the great multitude—a car so low in price that no man making a good salary will be unable to own one." The car had to be lightweight, strong, and economical. At a race in Florida, on a wrecked French racer, Ford had seen a lightweight, heavy-duty steel alloy that contained vanadium. That was the metal he would use for car parts that would get a lot of hard use. He would make the cylinder heads removable so that it would be easier to maintain and repair the engine. And, instead of putting the steering and controls on the right as in other cars, he would put them on the left. The body would be ex-

Ford was one of the most influential figures in the development of the automobile. He led the industry in building affordable, high-quality vehicles.

actly the same for all cars. To keep painting simple and cheap, customers could have a car painted in the color of their choice, so long as that color was black. On September 24, 1908, the car was introduced. For the next 19 years, it was the only car Ford made.

Ford called the car Model T. Others nicknamed it "Tin Lizzie" because it looked so fragile. It was an open car powered by a four-cylinder, 20-horse-power engine. It had two forward speeds, a reverse controlled by pedals, and three foot pedals—the main clutch, the footbrake, and the gear changer. At first, the Model T sold for $850. Windshield, top, headlights, speedometer, and spare tire all cost extra. Soon, though, Ford found ways to lower the price to under $300. Most comparable cars cost $2,000 or $3,000, which was beyond the means of the average worker, who made about $500 a year. The Model T was efficient, reliable, moderate in price, and easy to fix. Owners could buy parts for it at their local dime stores and at Sears.

Ford made sure the Model T got publicity. He sent eight of them to auto shows in Europe and advertised them in the widely read *Saturday Evening Post* magazine. By the end of 1910, the Ford Motor Company was recognized far and wide as the leader in building affordable, high-quality automobiles. But Ford had a problem. He could not produce enough Model T's to keep up with the demand. He had to find a new, better, faster way to build cars. He thought he could make cars more cheaply by buying firms that made the parts he needed instead of paying someone outside his company for these parts. Like Leland, he made sure parts were interchangeable. Then he went one step further,

THE MODEL T

The Ford Motor Company introduced the Model T in 1908. It became the first automobile produced using modern assembly line techniques. Inexpensive yet sturdy, the Model T was, in Henry Ford's words, "a motor car for the great multitude." In 1919, about half of the automobiles in the world were Model T Fords. By 1927, when the last Model T was produced, more than 15 million had been sold.

Model T included many of the best features of the other automobiles plus a few new ideas. The four-cylinder engine used little fuel, yet produced enough power for the car to reach a top speed of 40 miles per hour. Because the engine had a simple design it was easy to service and repair. The fuel tank was located under the front seat rather than farther forward where it would reduce leg room. The coils that controlled ignition, or starting the engine, were mounted in a box on the dashboard for easy access. In addition, the Model T had three foot pedals. One controlled the brakes, one allowed the car to reverse, and the third gave the car two forward speeds. To prevent overheating, water in the radiator was cooled by a fan driven by the engine. The exhaust pipe was fitted with a muffler to reduce engine noise.

Ford's assembly line production process revolutionized the way cars were manufactured. The assembly line allowed Ford to build an entire car in about 90 minutes.

developing a moving assembly line. Others before Ford had used an assembly process, but he revolutionized it.

Ford changed the way cars were made. In 1912 he set up small teams of workers at different stations in the plant. These teams built complete cars using parts made and assembled at other stations. The next year, Ford began experimenting with a moving assembly line, a power-driven conveyor system. The conveyor belt carried the gradually assembled car at the proper height and speed from one work station to another. Each worker performed only one part of a job, adding just one component to the new car as it passed by the workstation.

At first, Ford used the system to assemble just one component of the car—a gadget called a magneto. Using the assembly line cut the amount of time required to assemble a magneto from 18 minutes to 5. By the end of 1914, Ford was using the system to assemble the entire car. Instead of taking 14 hours to build a Model T, the process took a little over 90 minutes, and

Ford was turning one out every 30 seconds of every workday. By 1919, Ford had plants in Europe as well as in America, and about half of all the motor vehicles in the world were Model T Fords.

A Transportation and Social Revolution

In 1895 most automobile factories were barns or sheds occupied by a mechanic and a few pieces of machinery. Ten years later, some of those barns and sheds had turned into factories operating assembly lines. By 1909, police cars, fire trucks, and mail delivery vehicles were common sights in some cities, and farmers using automobiles were getting crops to market faster and more cheaply than before.

The automobile changed the landscape, society, and the way of life. Slowly the automobile was replacing the horse. In an advertisement for one of his cars, Ransom Olds explained why: the car never "kicks or bites, never tires on long runs, and never sweats in hot weather. It does not require care in the stable and only eats while on the road." Industries that depended on the horse—blacksmiths, stables, carriage makers—saw their trade falling off. Some went out of business. Others shifted their operation to automobiles. New industries and markets opened up—automobile showrooms, auto body and parts manufacturers, service stations, and public

Fire engines powered by internal combustion engines became a common sight in many cities by 1913, when this photograph was taken.

The automobile industry inspired dozens of other business ideas. New car showrooms (above) displayed the latest models available for purchase; service stations (left) opened for repairs, storage, and sales.

garages. The first garage in the United States—"a stable for renting, sale, storage, and repair of motor vehicles"—opened in 1899. It was just a matter of time until someone came up with hand-cranked gasoline fuel pumps and traffic lights with red and green glass disks and a buzzer. Special magazines were published. Special accessories were advertised. No motorist wanted to be without the Collapsible Rubber Auto Wash Basin, used to "remedy the soiled condition of the hands after making adjustments or repairs on the road." Clothing for motorists became big business. Motorists needed clothes that would protect them from the dust when it was dry, the rain when it was wet, and the wind at all times. They rushed to buy goggles, coats called dusters that covered the wearer from neck to ankle, hats, caps, gloves, scarves, leggings, and foot warmers. Not just any clothing would do. Magazines like *The Automobile* and *Motor*

Age published articles with titles like "What the Well-Dressed Autoist Now Wears" and "How to Stay Stylish in an Open Car."

In America especially, the automobile brought change. When Henry Ford priced the automobile low enough to be affordable to the average worker, he raised working Americans to a new level of respect, one that used to belong only to the wealthy. The automobile gave Americans a freedom, flexibility, and mobility they had not had before. Rural Americans especially felt the effects. Now they could escape the loneliness and isolation of the farm more frequently. Instead of going to the city once a week, on the weekend, they could go every day if they wanted. They did not have to make everything themselves. They could buy clothes, tools, and other items in stores in towns.

In war, as in peace, the automobile had an impact. The day after Britain declared war on Germany in 1914, the British government asked people to volunteer their motor vehicles to use in the war—for transport, as ambulances, as patrol cars, as fighting vehicles. The government did not think that the thousands of vehicles offered were enough. So the War Department marched into the British Daimler plant, which was closed for a holiday, seized every motor vehicle in sight, and stenciled the initials "WD" (for War Depart-

Fashion-conscious car owners dressed in high style, wearing specially designed coats, hats, goggles, and scarves.

English volunteers line up for inspection in front of their vehicles in 1917 as part of the war effort. Civilians offered their automobiles for service as ambulances, patrol cars, cargo transport, and even fighting vehicles.

ment) on the side of each. In France, 600 taxis were seized by the military governor of Paris to rush troops to the front. This was just the first of many motorized transports used in the war. Automobiles carried several hundred thousand soldiers and hundreds of thousands of tons of supplies to the besieged town of Verdun in France. For weeks, an unbroken stream of vehicles navigated their precious cargoes along the Sacred Way, the only communication road left open in the battle area. The most used car in the war was the Model T. The British alone had 19,000. By the time the war was over, there was no doubt that the automobile was here to stay.

The Age of the Automobile

While World War I was raging, manufacturers were too busy turning out war supplies to think about producing automobiles for private use. Demand was down anyway, because fuel was in short supply and luxury goods like automobiles were being taxed. But when the war ended, there was a new demand for cars, especially large and expensive ones. Automobiles, taxis, and buses again began to appear on the streets of Europe. The daring deeds of race car drivers found their way into the sports pages of European newspapers. In the United States, the automobile ceased to be just a handy way to get from one place to another faster. It became an indispensable part of daily life in a nation that went automobile crazy.

Special Cars for Privileged People

In the early years, engineers and inventors had not been too concerned about how an automobile looked or how elegant and stylish it was. They were interested in the engine and how well the vehicle performed. But in the early 1900s, before World War I, there were many very rich people both in Europe and in the United States. The automobile was a symbol of their social status, a sign of wealth they could show off any place or any time they chose. Wealthy Europeans, in fact, were advised to have more than one car. That way, they would be sure to have the right car for each circumstance, one with a body made just for them by the finest coachmakers, featuring velvet, brocade, and leather interiors and thick pile carpets. The wealthy bought these cars. But they did not drive them. Instead, they hired professional chauffeurs. As one very rich woman explained, "I am not concerned in the least with the motor. I leave that to Monsieur Chauffeur. My only interest is the interior."

The first luxury car was unveiled in

An advertisement for the Great Arrow automobile, a status symbol for the wealthy.

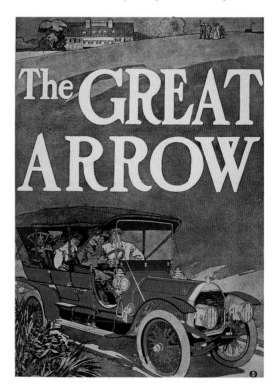

The Daimler Company's Mercedes line offered luxury, style, speed, and prestige—all of which appealed to wealthy car buyers.

1901 in Nice, France. The car had been made by the Daimler Company but was called Mercedes after the young daughter of an Austro-Hungarian businessman and diplomat named Emil Jellinek. He was the one who had persuaded Daimler to make a new kind of automobile, one that was long, low, and fast. Never before had there been a car quite like this one. It was everything Jellinek had asked for and more. With its steel body, special mechanism to make shifting gears easier, unique radiator that looked like the honeycomb of a bee, four speeds plus reverse, and average speed of 35 miles an hour, the Mercedes set new standards of elegance and performance. Even though it cost more than $2,000, rich Europeans rushed to

buy it. They did not care how much it cost. The car was beautiful and powerful and innovative and they wanted it.

A few years later, in Britain, a 41-year-old electrical engineer named Henry Royce created a car that came to be known as the "most famous luxury car of them all." Royce had bought his own first car in 1903. Plagued by one mechanical problem after another, he soon became disgusted with the French-made vehicle. Rather than try to fix this car, Royce decided to build his own. In 1906 Royce went into partnership with the Honorable Charles S. Rolls, a young British aristocrat who was selling Panhard cars. That year, at an auto show in Britain, they introduced the Silver Ghost Rolls Royce. It was called *Silver Ghost* because of its shiny aluminum-painted body and silver-plated metalwork and because it was so quiet when it was running. When he built the car, Royce was not looking for the new or different or for spectacular performance. He was the first to admit that there were no innovations on this car. "I invent nothing," he said. He took the best features of other cars and used them to their best advantage. The car, which soon won the reputation of being "the best car in the world," was also the most expensive. Elegance, beauty, and quality had been its creator's goals. Only the highest quality parts were used, and only the most skilled craftspeople contributed their labor. Each part of the car was hand-polished. And, to make sure there was not even the tiniest blemish anywhere, each part was examined through a magnifying glass. The Silver Ghost was a triumph, one that Rolls Royce kept producing for almost 20 years.

In America, too, comfort and elegance were becoming more important.

The cars exhibited at the New York auto show in 1905 were an example. The focus was less on speed and more on style and comfort—doors, canopy tops, longer bodies, attention to detail. There was even a new kind of air-filled tire that helped a car travel faster and made for a safer and more comfortable ride than was possible with solid rubber tires. At the 1910 show, some cars had bodies shaped like a torpedo. The sides of these cars were raised to shelter and safeguard the driver, and the dashboard was moved forward. By the time the 1915 show rolled around, Olds was offering glass windshields and tops as standard equipment. That was the year the California top—complete with side curtains and celluloid windows—appeared, to the delight of automobile enthusiasts everywhere.

The Motoring Revolution

By the 1920s, the automobile was more popular—and more necessary—than ever before. Young people especially wanted to put war behind, to escape into a world of fun and games. People were willing to sacrifice to buy a car. That car, of course, had to be powerful, elegant, of high quality, and luxurious. The auto became a means of escape and, along with movies, represented one of the most popular pastimes. Hollywood movies did much to spread the image of fashionably dressed men and women enjoying themselves in powerful, luxurious cars. Movie stars loved posing with their extravagant automobiles. "The bigger the star, the bigger the car," went one saying. The car of

Hollywood filmmaker Mack Sennett captured the fashionable image of the car in his silent films featuring the Bathing Beauties.

The luxurious Duesenberg is displayed in a showroom window. Its manufacturer billed it as a car "for people of long established culture and wealth."

choice of the rich and famous was generally a Mercedes, a Rolls, a Hispano Suiza, or a Duesenberg.

The Hispano Suiza was truly a European car, designed in Switzerland and built in Paris. The latest technology had been used in creating it, technology that had been used to make airplane engines in World War I. The Duesenberg was an American car, the creation of two German-born brothers, Frederick and August Duesenberg. Frederick, who had taught himself automotive engineering, began building racing cars in Indianapolis after World War I. In 1926 the brothers fulfilled a dream—to build the most luxurious car. According to advertisements for the 1928 model, the Duesenberg was "for people of long established culture and wealth, possessing the inevitable good taste which accompanies these two characteristics and the

inclination to cater to it." No car had ever been built in the United States to compare with it. It did not even carry an identifying nameplate like other cars. It was so extraordinary that it did not need one. Owning a Duesenberg signified wealth and position. What other auto had its styling, its cocktail cabinets for passengers in the backseat, its luxurious upholsteries, or such splendid gadgets as an altimeter that measured heights?

By the mid-1920s, the auto had changed greatly. Many cars came with balloon wheels and bodies that were lower and totally enclosed. Closed cars became more popular than open ones. Car paints of different colors were developed, and cars appeared in bold new hues. The star of the 1924 auto shows was a light blue Oldsmobile. In 1927 almost a million people lined up before

The Roadster, as pictured in a 1930s Ford catalog, is described as "a car for Youth and Country Club." It offered an optional rumble seat, an extra seat installed in the rear of the car.

dawn in front of Ford's New York headquarters just to see the bright new cars unveiled. Autos sported shiny metal accessories and gadgets galore. Lamps and radiators with glossy nickel-plated finishes became standard equipment, and many tires had white sidewalls.

Powerful new "sports" cars with huge engines, tested on the racetrack and made to be driven fast, caught people's fancy. Some even had superchargers, or "blowers," that boosted power even more by forcing extra fuel into the engine. Amateur mechanics on both sides of the Atlantic wanted to make their cars perform better. One of the favorite ways to do this was by playing with the carburetor. Since an engine did not run well unless gasoline was fed in the finest of sprays and mixed with just the right amount of air, most cars depended on some form of carburetor to feed the engine. Gasoline additives appeared for the first time, and cars be-

gan to run on gasoline with lead added in different ratios or "octane" ratings.

All through the 1920s and into the 1930s, luxury cars abounded, especially in the United States. Millions of Americans owned their own cars. When asked why she and her husband had bought a car when they did not have a bathtub, one farm woman replied that it was simple—you could not drive to town in a bathtub. By 1928, so many Americans had bought cars that automakers were starting to worry about the market. Cars were beginning to look a lot alike, and people had begun buying them used instead of new. By 1930, 77 percent of all the cars registered worldwide were registered in the United States, and 85 percent of all cars were produced by U.S. automakers.

In the rest of the world, however, most people could not afford to buy a car until late in the 1920s, if then. In Europe, many manufacturers copied

WHAT DOES THE CARBURETOR DO?

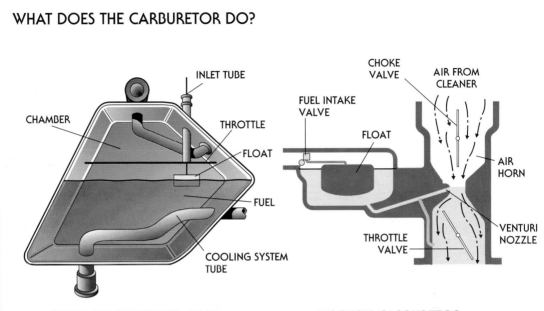

SURFACE VAPORIZER-1890s

MODERN CARBURETOR

The internal combustion engine produces power by burning a mixture of fuel and air. For maximum efficiency, the air and fuel must be mixed in exact proportions, ideally one part of fuel for fifteen parts of air.

Early automobile engineers used a device known as a surface vaporizer to mix the fuel with air. The surface vaporizer heats the liquid fuel until the molecules near the surface evaporate and mix with the air in the chamber. The fuel is heated by a tube connected to the engine's cooling system. The cooling system flushes hot water through the tube. This heats the tube and the fuel in which it is submerged.

When the throttle opens, the air and fuel vapors escape from the chamber through the inlet tube and enter the engine cylinder. Once inside the cylinder, the air and fuel vapors are compressed by the piston and ignited by the spark plug, creating power to run the engine.

Because its efficiency depended on the temperature of the fuel, the surface vaporizer did not work as well when the engine was cold as it did when the engine was hot. It also did not work as well in cold climates as it did in warm ones. For better performance at all temperatures, engineers devised the carburetor, which uses air pressure, rather than heat, to mix the fuel and air into a fine mist.

Fuel enters the carburetor through the intake valve. The fuel in the carburetor is kept at a constant level by the float, which automatically closes the intake valve when the carburetor is full. When the driver presses on the accelerator pedal, the throttle valve opens and air rushes through the air horn. The choke controls the amount of air entering the air horn. Suction from the rushing air draws fuel through the Venturi nozzle. When the droplets of fuel hit the rushing air, they are broken up into a fine mist. This mist is drawn into the cylinders and burned to power the engine.

Millions of Americans owned cars by the 1930s. Here, parked cars crowd the main street of a California town.

American production techniques but offered a greater variety of designs from which to pick. As American cars got bigger, European cars got smaller. In 1930 the number of private cars on the road in Britain finally exceeded 1 million. In France and Germany, that did not happen until after World War II. Russia did not produce its first private car until 1926. In the 1930s, middle-class families in Europe started buying cars for the first time. The cars they bought were not luxury cars. They were closed cars that could be used year round—plain little sedans with small engines. They were not made for speed or performance, and they did not cost major sums of money. They were designed to be solid family cars, with upright bodies and enough space inside to accommodate family members on closed-in seats.

In the United States, style still was all-important. How a car looked often meant more than how well it was built. Competition was fierce: to fight it and the growing used-car market, automakers started changing car styles a little each year. They wanted to make the previous year's models outdated enough to tempt people to buy new ones. In general, cars of the 1930s were more comfortable and easier to drive

Style was important to many American car buyers. A 1930 Lincoln catalog boasts that this Sport Phaeton "is a car of unusual attractiveness."

Motorists take advantage of a sunny Colorado day by driving through the mountains in their Ford automobile.

than earlier models. Many had four-wheel brakes, headlights, and trunks where travelers could stow their luggage. Oil and acetylene gas lamps had been replaced by bright electric lights. And, thanks to an American named Paul Galvin, cars could be equipped with radios at reasonable prices. By the end of the 1930s, automatic directional signals and automatic transmissions were also available. With automatic transmission, drivers no longer had to choose the right gear to use because the automobile did it for them.

Times were hard for most people in the 1930s. The world was in a deep economic depression. The rich and famous still bought cars and went touring in Europe, but even the most luxurious cars were selling at surprisingly low prices. With most people struggling just to feed their families, a new car was a sign of wealth and prestige. Yet, people clung to their cars even when they could not afford gasoline. The car was their means of escape. As long as they owned a car, they could physically get away from their problems. In America especially, thousands took to the road—some for a vacation, some looking for excitement and adventure, but most hoping to find work and a better life. "Buy a car," pleaded one poster. "Help bring back prosperity. When you buy an automobile you give three months work to someone, which allows him to buy other products."

By the 1940s, the depression was in the past and the world was once again at war. Production of automobiles for private use slowed down and then came to a stop. Once again, the automobile played a major role in a war. The American jeep and the German Kübelwagen, or bucket car, became familiar sights in war-torn Europe and Africa.

New Mobility, New Ways of Life

By the 1940s, the automobile had changed how and where people lived, worked, shopped, and spent their time.

It had set in motion a chain reaction that showed no signs of stopping. More cars, for example, led to more and better roads. Once people had cars and the highways on which to drive them, they traveled more often and went to more places. Since most roads were not well marked, motorists needed maps to keep from getting lost. Detailed road maps became best sellers, as vital as a set of tools. Parking lots, garages, and automatic traffic lights began to appear in cities and towns.

Roadside businesses cropped up to serve motorists' needs. The first modern filling station had opened in 1913. By 1929, there were more than 100,000. Before long, other businesses began to appear next to the filling stations—places where the tired motorist could sleep and the hungry motorist could eat. In the United States, the first tourist cabins appeared after World War I. Not much later—in 1924—an innkeeper in California came up with a new name for his roadside inn. He

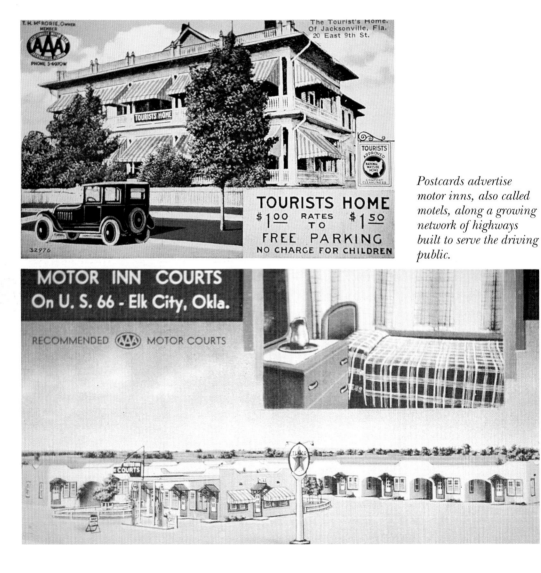

Postcards advertise motor inns, also called motels, along a growing network of highways built to serve the driving public.

The drive-in restaurant flourished as car owners grew increasingly fond of ordering and eating an occasional meal in the car.

called it a motel. That same year, an enterprising Floridian opened a new kind of restaurant, a "drive-in," where motorists could order, receive, and eat their food without having to get out of their cars.

The word *vacation* took on a new meaning. Now that cars made it possible for people to go farther from home, they wanted to spend less time at work. Business owners began taking more time off, especially in summer. Slowly they began allowing people who worked for them to do the same. A new form of recreation became popular—autocamping. Car dealers said it strengthened the

A woman relaxes at a campsite in Yellowstone National Park in 1920. National parks in the United States attracted millions of visitors who packed tents and other necessities for car-camping vacations.

A 1930s luxury Lincoln had a separate seat for a chauffeur and a covered compartment in back where passengers could travel in comfort and privacy.

family. Millions believed this, packed their tents, and headed for the open countryside. It was only a matter of time before some people began to hitch trailers and mobile homes to their cars. Tourism had been important in Europe for a long time. By the mid-1930s, it was the third largest industry in the United States as well. Among America's most popular vacation spots were its national parks. Not many people had been able to visit them before because most parks were off the beaten track. The automobile changed that. Remote spots were no longer so remote.

Automakers began gearing many of their advertisements and sales pitches toward women. Because of the self-starter, more women were driving than ever before. Eventually, this trend helped change clothing styles. Full-skirted, floor-length dresses got in the way when women were behind the wheel. So they replaced them with shorter, less full outfits that did not interfere with driving.

Another reason women became targets was the automakers' tendency to believe the saying, "Men buy cars, women choose them."

In America, more than anywhere else, the automobile revolutionized society. In the years between the end of World War I and 1927, the number of concrete roads in the United States had grown from 7,000 miles to 50,000 miles. By then, Americans owned four out of five of the world's cars. By the 1920s, the auto industry was the largest in the nation. It used so much steel, glass, wood, gasoline, and rubber that it provided jobs for millions. It was the backbone of the economy, and it changed American buying and selling habits. In 1911 one automaker, Studebaker, had announced that people who bought one of their cars did not have to pay in a lump sum. Instead, they could "buy now, pay later." In less than a decade, more than half of all the cars sold in the United States were sold on time payments. By then, people could buy other goods "on time" as well.

The automobile changed American living patterns. People who owned cars no longer had to live in the city just because they happened to work there. They could drive to work if they wanted. Many city residents began to build and buy houses outside the congested cities, in areas called suburbs. Recognizing that there were sales to be made in the suburbs, shops and other small businesses opened there, giving birth to a new kind of shopping area—the shopping center.

The effect of the automobile in America was one of the topics of a book written by two sociologists, Robert S. Lynde and Helen Merrell Lynde, about a small Indiana town in the mid-1920s. Included in the book, *Middletown: A Study in Contemporary American Culture,* were these comments:

[The automobile upset such time-honored habits and attitudes as] "Rain or shine, I never miss a Sunday morning at church"; "A high-school boy does not need much spending money"; "I don't need exercise, walking to the office keeps me fit"; "I wouldn't think of moving out of town and being so far from my friends"; "Parents ought always to know where their children are.". . .

"We'd rather do without clothes than give up the car," said one mother of nine children. "We used to go to his sister's to visit, but by the time we'd get the children shoed and dressed there wasn't any money left for carfare. Now, no matter how they look, we just poke 'em in the car and take 'em along."

Many families feel that an automobile is justified as an agency holding the family group together. "I never feel as close to my family as when we are all together in the car," said one business class mother. . . .

The Auto—Friend and Foe

During World War II, manufacturers had stopped producing cars for civilians to make way for production of military goods. But once the war was over, automakers geared up to produce more commercial cars than ever before. They started out to put returning veterans and their families behind the wheels of cars that were safe and practical and did not cost too much for the average person. They soon progressed to a broader goal—putting at least one car in every driveway. Different approaches were taken in different parts of the world to accomplish this.

Small Is Better

European automakers were faced with multiple challenges after the war. Many of their factories were in ruins and had to be totally rebuilt. Selling cars was not a problem. Building them fast enough was. The war-ravaged Europeans wanted cars but could not afford to spend a lot of money on them. Since gasoline was still rationed—and would remain so until 1950—the cars had to be fuel efficient. So, to attract customers, automakers designed lower priced cars that could go a fair distance on a liter of gasoline.

Within a few years, many European auto factories had become highly mechanized employers of tens of thousands of workers. At the same time, they had made many improvements to the auto-

mobile, including disk brakes and direct fuel injection. Disk brakes consist of small pads that grip both sides of an iron disk attached to each wheel. In a fuel injection system, a small pump delivers exactly the right amount of gasoline to the engine. One major technical development, the introduction of the Wankel rotary engine, named after Dr. Felix Wankel, the German who helped create it, occurred in 1954. Instead of pistons and valves, this engine has a pair of triangular parts called rotors. These rotors turn inside a chamber, and in so doing they take in and compress the gases in each part of the chamber. The rotary engine was more dependable, smaller, and lighter than the standard engine of the day, and it used less fuel.

By the early 1950s, there were so many unsafe cars on the roads of Europe that some people became concerned about highway safety. Campaigns were begun to address the growing problem, and European automakers spent time and money seeking solutions. One of their approaches was to find ways to make cars bigger on the inside (so they would stay comfortable) but smaller outside (so traffic and congestion would be reduced). One of the smallest cars European automakers came up with was the "bubble" car. The two-seater Italian Isetta, which appeared in the 1950s, was not much longer than a bicycle, looked like a three-wheeler, and had an enormous front door.

THE WANKEL ROTARY ENGINE

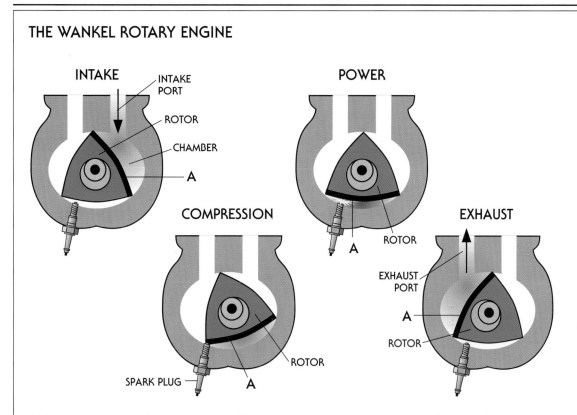

INTAKE
- INTAKE PORT
- ROTOR
- CHAMBER
- A

POWER
- ROTOR
- A

COMPRESSION
- ROTOR
- A
- SPARK PLUG

EXHAUST
- EXHAUST PORT
- A
- ROTOR

Although piston engines are powerful and efficient they consist of many moving parts. The greater the number of parts, the greater the chances for a part to break or malfunction. Many engineers sought to design a simpler engine that used a revolving, or rotary, design. The most successful of these was designed by Felix Wankel in 1929. In place of several pistons that moved up and down within cylinders, Wankel designed a single, three-sided piston, or rotor, that rotates in clockwise direction within an oval chamber. Like piston engines, the Wankel engine uses a four-stroke cycle:

Intake As the rotor turns, one side sweeps past the intake port. A partial vacuum, or sucking action, pulls a mixture of fuel and air vapors through the intake port and into the chamber. When side A passes the intake port, the mixture of air

and fuel vapors is trapped within the chamber.

Compression As the rotor continues turning in a clockwise direction the molecules of air and fuel are forced into a smaller space inside the chamber. As the mixture of air and fuel vapors compresses, it heats up.

Power At the moment when the air and fuel mixture is most compressed, the spark plug fires. The spark ignites the air and fuel vapors, causing them to burn inside the chamber. The burning vapors expand rapidly, driving the rotor around the chamber and powering the crankshaft, which powers the wheels.

Exhaust When side A sweeps past the exhaust port, the burned vapors rush out of the chamber. The trailing tip pushes the last of the exhaust out of the chamber, and the four-stroke cycle begins again.

Potential buyers gather around a Volkswagen Beetle at the German Industrial Exposition in New York City around 1950.

In response to the "bubble" car came the British "mini," the first small car that really seated four people. In the 1959 Morris Mini, the engine was turned sideways, the wheels were tiny, and the suspension—the part that supports the car—was made of rubber. Because of these modifications, most of the inside space could be used for passengers. Almost every small car produced since then has been very similar in design. Some people called the car a "roller-skate for those who can't afford to run a car." Many complained that every time it rained the ignition system was drowned, that the door hinges kept breaking off, and that the driver could not see the speedometer because the steering wheel was in the way. But, at the same time, four people could fit more comfortably into the Morris Mini than into many bigger cars. And, it performed better than a lot of sports cars.

The most popular small car of all time came from Germany. It was the Volkswagen "Beetle," and more of them have been made than any other car. The story of the Beetle actually began in 1934, when German leader Adolf Hitler announced that a *Volksauto,* "a people's car," would be built. He invited Professor Ferdinand Porsche Sr. to Berlin and told him to design and make prototypes, or models, of such a car. Four years later, production was under way, and many cars had been ordered and paid for by German citizens. But the war intervened, and the would-be car owners' money went to produce military equipment instead. The car Hitler had promised was not introduced until 1945. By then, the plant in Wolfsburg that produced it was under British control, and it remained so for the next several years. The Beetle was small, efficient, sturdy, and cheap, and it ran well.

It gave many German families their first chance to go driving. No one had expected the little car that looked like a giant bug to become so popular that it would inspire contests to see how many people could cram into it or be the star of Hollywood movies. But it did, and at the height of its production, 5,000 Beetles were rolling off the assembly line each day for shipment to more than 100 countries.

The American Way

World War II had limited what Americans could buy and what they could do. When the war was over, they could not wait to buy all kinds of things. With more than half of the 26 million cars in the nation at least 10 years old, the first thing many Americans wanted to buy was a car. The demand was so great that the orders began piling up. To help meet the demand, new auto manufacturing companies emerged. These companies were known as independents because they were not associated with the nation's three big automakers—Ford, General Motors, and Chrysler, which had come into being in 1925.

The American people wanted big, stylish cars, and they wanted to be comfortable when they traveled, especially over long distances. They viewed cars much as they had in the 1920s—as symbols of success, social status, and taste. "Build 'em big and beautiful and as fast as you can" became the motto of American automakers. The result was automobiles that looked good but were sometimes lacking in safety or efficiency. What one carmaker did, another soon copied. In 1948, for example, Cadillac came out with twin tail fins. For several years after, most American cars had tail fins. By the early 1950s, big-engined, large, brightly colored cars with lots of shiny chrome were the American dream. Later, that changed, largely because America became involved in war in Korea. Military requirements affected the amount of fuel available and the kind and amount of materials that could be used for auto production.

For Americans, the 1950s was the decade of the automobile. Auto dealers sold 58 million cars. Congress authorized the building of more than 40,000 miles of highway to link all the major cities in the nation. This meant more traffic. But it also meant more jobs and greater prosperity. One out of every six U.S. workers had a job that had to do with four-wheel travel. Some worked on roads. Others staffed assembly lines.

Sparkling new 1955 Buicks, Oldsmobiles, and Pontiacs await delivery after coming off the assembly line at a General Motors plant.

Ford shows off its large, stylish 1949 models (above). The 1946 Pontiac (below) is so roomy a child can stand in it.

Still others sold insurance. People had more leisure time, and they spent a lot of it working on, playing with, or going somewhere in their automobiles. The landscape became a panorama of neon signs and huge posterboard cutouts meant to lure passing motorists into restaurants, motels, and shops. In Illinois, a man named Ray Kroc opened the world's first McDonald's and set off a "come as you are, eat in your car" fast-food revolution.

Now that more people had cars and there were more highways on which to travel, the move away from the big cities accelerated. By the end of the decade, one-third of all Americans lived in the suburbs. Most suburbs, however, had little or no public transportation. A person could not get along without at least one car, and most families had two.

HOW THE AUTOMOBILE WORKS

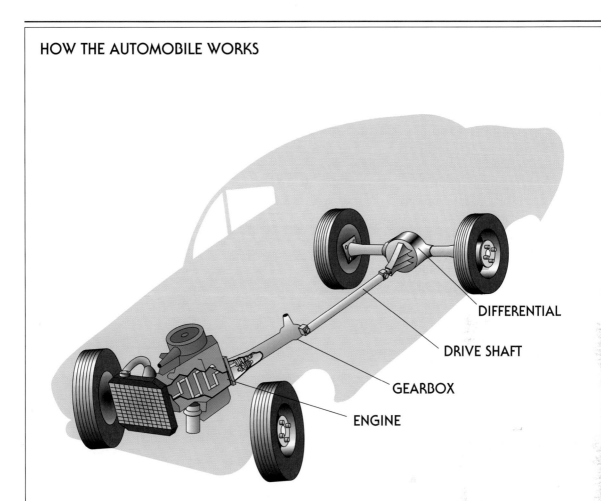

DIFFERENTIAL

DRIVE SHAFT

GEARBOX

ENGINE

Most modern automobiles have four basic systems that allow them to move under their own power. These four systems are the engine, the gearbox or transmission, the drive shaft, and the differential. The typical car, with its engine mounted in front, feeds power to the back wheels through the gearbox, drive shaft, and differential.

This process begins within the engine, where the crankshaft turns at a constant speed. The typical engine works best when the crankshaft makes 2,000 to 5,000 revolutions per minute.

The crankshaft is connected to the gearbox. Inside the gearbox are gears of different sizes. The revolving crankshaft turns the gears. The gears rotate at different speeds. Each gear speed changes the revolutions per minute—either slowing them down or speeding them up—as they progress through the gearbox to the drive shaft.

The drive shaft is connected to the gearbox at one end and to the differential at the other. It transmits the revolving, or rotary, motion from the gearbox to the differential. The differential transmits power to the wheels, allowing the wheels to move.

Most men had jobs in the city and needed a car to get to work. Most women were homemakers. They needed their own cars—to do errands, to go shopping, and to chauffeur their children from school to doctor and dentist appointments and to social and athletic functions.

Over the next few decades, American attitudes about the automobile, automobile safety, and the effects of the automobile on society and on the environment went through a series of changes. There were many reasons for this, including changes in the economy and in the environment, the rising price and dwindling supply of fuel, and competition from auto manufacturers in Japan and other countries. By the mid-1960s, Americans were growing more unhappy with the quality, size, and cost of American-made cars. "Nineteen-hundred sixty-five was the peak," said one expert, "and the cars . . . seemed to go downhill from then. The engines got bigger, not better, the paint became wilder, and the knobs fell off the dash."

Americans wanted—and needed—smaller, more efficient, better-made cars, and they turned to foreign manufacturers to get them. Cars made by the Toyota Motor Company of Japan captured their attention. The company's

The 1950s was the decade of the car in the United States. Americans demanded comfort and style and carmakers responded with cars like the 1951 two-seater convertible LeSabre (left). The growing number of cars required new highways. A portion of the new Hollywood-Santa Ana Freeway in Southern California is shown in 1954 (above).

A 1965 Pontiac car exhibit. Some car experts say the quality of American-made cars declined after that year.

founder, Kiichiro Toyoda, had visited automobile factories in the United States in the 1930s. A few years later, he had begun mass producing cars in his own factory—copied from one he had visited in Detroit. After World War II, with the support of the Japanese government, Toyoda had once again begun producing cars, using new technical and engineering skills.

By 1980, for most Americans, big, gas-guzzling cars were a thing of the past. Toyota was the leading seller of cars in the United States. Not too many years after that Japan, not America, was the world's leading automobile producer.

The Auto Takes a Toll

Over the years, the automobile changed the world, and the people as well. Not all the changes, though, have been good for society or for the environment. In some cases, as the number of cars multiplied, so did the problems.

Nicholas Cugnot, for example, did not hurt himself or anyone else that fateful eighteenth-century day when he ran his steam wagon into a wall. Then, and for many years after, self-propelled vehicles were oddities, few and far between. But by the early 1900s, this was no longer the case. And, by the 1920s,

Toyota trucks are unloaded from ships in Baltimore, Maryland, in 1981. The Japanese automaker, Toyota, was the leading seller of cars in the United States by 1980.

the automobile was an important part of life. Because it played such a major role in the economy, not much was done to regulate or control it. No one had to take a driving test or have auto insurance before getting behind the wheel. Most automobiles did not have bumpers or brake lights or any other safety accessories. National government left the subject of traffic control strictly to local police and others. In Paris, the traffic situation was so bad that the head of the metropolitan police pronounced it "insoluble."

By the 1930s, more than 30,000 people were being killed in car accidents each year in the United States alone. In Britain in 1934, four years after all speed limits there had been lifted, the minister of transport described road deaths as "a hideous and growing blot on our national life." Not until the 1950s, however, did people really become concerned about automobile and roadway safety and efficiency. And, by then, both in Europe and in the United States, the roadways, of which there were too few, were full of unsafe cars.

Traffic jams and parking problems were another major issue. As more families became car owners, more people chose to travel on their own. They wanted to drive their own cars to work, not ride with someone else. Because road building and improvements did not keep up with the growing number of vehicles, roads were quickly becoming overloaded. By the 1950s, for example, traffic passing in and around London had doubled. By the early 1960s, it was not unusual for traffic to be bottled up for as much as 25 miles at a stretch in England. Conditions were as bad or worse in Paris, in Tokyo, and in some

Junked and abandoned cars litter the roadway. Scenes like this have prompted concerns about how cars affect the environment.

American cities. The smaller cars designed and produced by European and Japanese automakers did not solve the problem. In Tokyo, for example, the parking problem got so serious that some people converted their apartments into parking lots. High-rise parking garages became a reality in many places.

The global environment was also affected—and still is. Cities and towns suffer from noise pollution, most of which is due to traffic. Deposits of asbestos ground from automobile brakes and rubber worn away from tires are washed from the roadways into streams, where they pollute the water. Automobiles that are wrecked or no longer can be made to run are abandoned along roadways or left lying in fields because people do not know a good way to dispose of them. Car exhausts release into the air such harmful pollutants as carbon monoxide, lead, and nitrogen oxides.

Pollutants released into the air by automobiles and by factories help trigger the greenhouse effect, the warming of the earth's atmosphere. And, when these pollutants combine with rainwater, they form acid rain, which poisons the waters of inland lakes and rivers, killing fish and wildlife; acid rain also eats away at stone and metal, damaging old buildings and weakening bridges. Nitrogen oxides stream out of tail pipes and, mixed with hydrocarbons, create smog, a foul-smelling, brown, smoky fog that is harmful to health, irritates the eyes, and turns trees and plants brown.

The automobile made it possible for people to escape, to travel when they wanted and where they wanted. And they did exactly that, millions of them. As a result, unspoiled countryside is now a rarity. Billboards, arrows, lights,

Rush-hour traffic on a Los Angeles freeway adds to smoggy conditions, making downtown buildings barely visible on some days.

flashing signs, and commercial strips multiplied along roadways and combined with litter and debris left behind by passengers in vanishing cars to scar the landscape. Cities, too, felt the effects, especially in the United States. Beginning in the 1920s, city dwellers who could afford to moved to the suburbs. Some businesses soon began to move as well. The poor had no choice but to stay where they were. Those who had worked for businesses that moved found themselves without jobs and poorer than before. Some lost their homes when badly planned highways cut through—and destroyed—their neighborhoods. In time, many urban areas became strictly business centers. Others became slums.

Mass transit also suffered. For many years, street cars had provided transportation. But when their tracks began to interfere with automobile traffic, the solution was to get rid of them. Trains began to disappear as well. When the number of people riding trains began to drop, the government cut the amount it spent on them. Trains and tracks started to decay. Because trains and tracks were not in good shape, even fewer people wanted to travel on them. Eventually, many trains simply stopped running.

Over time, efforts have been made to deal with all the problems created by the automobile. Concern about automobile accidents and deaths led to campaigns like the British "Keep Death off the Roads" crusade and to new traffic and motor vehicle safety laws. In the United States, for example, a federal agency, the National Highway Traffic Safety Administration, was established. One of its tasks was to reduce car accidents by setting safety standards for all cars sold in the nation. Safety concerns also stimulated automotive safety designs, including seat belts, locks that prevent car doors from flying open in a crash, sturdy bumpers, and air bags that inflate almost upon impact. Overpasses and new roadways have been built to ease traffic congestion. In some cities, certain areas have been set aside strictly for pedestrians; automobiles are not allowed to enter at all. Laws have been passed and automotive improvements have been made to help bring about cleaner air and safer roads. Many cities have taken steps to lure back residents, businesses, and shoppers. And, in some European and Asian countries, new forms of mass transit have become popular. Still, problems brought on by the automobile have not been fully resolved. Since people worldwide cannot—or will not—do without automobiles, experts today continue to look for new and better ways to build and use these popular vehicles.

Forward to the Future

Only a little more than 100 years have passed since the first car made to be sold to the public rolled out of Karl Benz's workshop. Since then, building automobiles has become the largest manufacturing activity in the world. If automakers keep producing cars at present levels, by the year 2000 more than 500 million cars will be on the roads of the world. What many of those cars should—and will—be like has been on the minds and the drawing boards of scientists, engineers, designers, and others everywhere. Some of their ideas already have been translated into concept cars, special models to be tested and put on display at auto shows for enthusiasts to inspect and admire. In time, many of the designs and engineering innovations in these cars are incorporated into the automobiles people buy.

The Automobile in a Changing World

Almost as soon as the car became a reality, the world changed and then changed again and again to accommodate it. The solution to the problem of too many cars on too few roads, for example, was not to produce fewer cars but to build more and more roads. Although people today have no intention of giving up their cars, they have started to recognize that the world no longer can afford to change itself to accommodate the automobile. The time has come for the automobile to do the accommodating.

Environmental problems have already led automakers all over the world to put greater effort into building less

Cars fill the lanes of a busy Atlanta, Georgia, interstate highway. Cities responded to the increasing number of cars on the roads by building more highways.

In an effort to reduce air pollution and dependence on foreign oil, private and government researchers work on energy alternatives. Here, a U.S. Department of Energy researcher tests a battery for an electric car.

wasteful, longer lasting, recyclable cars. In recent years, many automakers have used lighter materials, such as plastics and aluminum, instead of steel. These materials make the cars more fuel efficient but, at the same time, they are harder to recycle than steel. And recycling has become a major issue. Most people agree that in the future cars must be designed in a way that makes it possible to recycle their parts and reuse their materials in new generations of cars. The metal parts of cars made by the German manufacturer Volkswagen already are 100 percent recyclable.

Noise pollution is also being addressed. Researchers are experimenting with mufflers that use electronics instead of physical materials to absorb sound. Automobiles are becoming sleeker and more streamlined. Automotive designers and engineers have been working on streamlining since the 1930s. The concept behind streamlining goes beyond style. It involves aerodynamics, which has to do with forces such as resistance and pressure applied by air or other gases in motion. The more streamlined a car, the less it resists the wind. And the less energy it uses to fight against the wind, the more fuel efficient it will be.

A Question of Fuel

Fuel is a major issue. Some nations are concerned about overdependence on foreign petroleum products, huge quantities of which go to fuel automobiles. Experts blame automobiles for up to two-thirds of all urban smog and one-quarter of the carbon dioxide in the air. All this has led governments to take action. The State of California, for example, is the single largest market for automobiles in the world. In 1990 California passed a law that applies to any automaker selling more than 5,000 vehicles a year in the state: beginning in 1998, at least 2 percent of cars sold in California must not release any pollution at all. By 2003, the figure will go from 2 percent to 10 percent. In 1992 the U.S. Senate passed an energy bill ordering that by the year 2000 government fleets of motor vehicles and most commercial fleets will use alternative fuels or electricity. The European Community and Japan are expected to come out with their own sets of regulations very soon.

One possible alternative fuel is ethanol, a form of alcohol that can be obtained by distilling such plants as sugar cane. Ethanol can be used by itself or mixed with gasoline to form a fuel called gasohol. Another possibility is hydrogen, which can be made from just about anything and is almost pollution free. The U.S. space shuttle has used hydrogen fuel cells to provide onboard electricity and drinking water. Hydrogen can be used in internal combustion engines. But if it is used instead to produce electricity in automotive fuel cells, it will take cars twice as far. Some European and Japanese automakers are working on hydrogen-fueled cars or already have prototypes that use hydrogen as fuel. One prototype produced by the Japanese manufacturer Mazda has a rotary-powered engine fueled by hydrogen and gives off water vapor instead of exhaust.

Some automakers are considering cars with more than one fuel system. A Volkswagen concept car uses batteries to run at low speeds and a two-cylinder gasoline engine to charge the batteries, accelerate, and run at higher speeds. The experimental Environmental Concept Car created by the Swedish automaker Volvo is made mostly of recyclable aluminum and runs on stored electricity or on a gas turbine engine powered by diesel fuel. Most experts agree that a practical hydrogen car and the basic installations and facilities to support it will come about—but not during this century.

The Mazda HR-X (left) runs on hydrogen, giving off water vapor instead of exhaust. The Volvo Environmental Concept Car (above) is made of recyclable aluminum and runs on stored electricity or diesel fuel.

The Electric Solution

Many people believe that the future will be the age of the electric car—not the electric auto of the past, but a new space-age machine that can hold its own against modern high-performance cars. One enthusiast can see the cars clearly: "They'll look like sleek jellybeans and be made of materials unheard of today. They'll be lighter and quieter than current cars." He goes on to predict that "Drivers will charge the vehicles' yet-to-be-developed batteries at home, potentially dooming gas stations." Some other people think that the first electric cars will be hybrids—electric-drive cars that use batteries but also use a small gasoline engine to recharge the batteries and make it possible for the car to go longer between charges. Still other people think that the system, not the car, will be a hybrid, with fast-moving, hydrogen-powered cars on major roadways and electric cars in cities where traffic is congested.

American, Japanese, and European automakers all have been working to be the first to produce a practical electric automobile, one that performs as well as a gasoline car. At first, they tried converting gasoline automobiles to electric, but that did not work very well. More recently, they have attempted to overcome major problems associated with the development of an electric car. One problem has been the electric motor. Engineers can design it to provide a car with acceleration. Or, they can design it to provide a car with power for steady operation at high speed. But designing an electric motor that will provide both yet still be light and not too costly has proved to be a challenge.

The central problem facing automakers trying to develop the electric car is creating a battery that can power a vehicle for long distances without needing to be recharged. Most of the batteries already developed have to be recharged every 100 miles or so. Recharging, however, may take an entire night. Another drawback is that the batteries will have to be replaced every two years or so—at a cost of about $1500.

Nissan's electric car has a lightweight battery that can be recharged in less than 15 minutes.

General Motors' electric car, Impact 3, accelerates from 0 to 60 mph in 8 seconds and has a range of 100 miles. It is expected to be ready for mass production by the end of the decade.

The drawbacks just mentioned have not ended interest in the electric car. The Japanese trade ministry wants to have at least 20,000 or more electric cars in use in Japan by the year 2000. One thousand electric vehicles are already being used on a trial basis by utilities and local governments there. The Japanese automaker Nissan has a prototype car with batteries weighing only half as much as the traditional ones and fully rechargeable in less than 15 minutes. General Motors has an electric concept car and expects to start commercial production in the late 1990s. The most unusual electric concept car, though, is a two-seater made by the French company, Renault. It is called *Zoom* and is perfect for small parking spaces. Bringing the rear wheels forward causes the rear of the car to rise, making the car "shrink" by almost 2 feet.

A Winning Partnership

In 1965 the head of a major American automobile manufacturing company made a speech about what the car would be like in 20 years. In a 1985 magazine article, he pointed out that although his predictions had been pretty much on target, there was one thing he—and everyone else—had underestimated. This was the microprocessor, the central element in most computers. No one knew that by 1985 most cars would have systems fully or partly controlled by computers.

Today, little computers called microchips are even more a part of the automobile than they were in 1985. Most cars have anywhere from 5 to 10 chips; some of the newest luxury models have as many as 50. The most power-

Many new cars rely on powerful microchip computers to control the engine and regulate the vital systems of the car.

ful chip controls the engine. Another calculates fuel efficiency and travel times. Some reduce exhaust emissions. Others control the firing of spark plugs, the devices in the cylinder of an internal combustion engine that give off the electrical sparks that ignite the fuel mixture. Still others provide the driver with information about engine temperature, fuel level, oil pressure, and the state of just about every system vital to the car.

In the early 1990s, visitors to Orlando, Florida, were given the opportunity to take part in a $12 million experiment by getting behind the wheel of a very special car—a "smart car." Engineers had created the smart car in the hope that it would help cut down on urban gridlock—city traffic jams so bad that no vehicle could move in any direction. The smart car had a hands-free cellular phone; a travel database listing

hundreds of hotels, motels, restaurants, and special events and attractions; and powerful twin microcomputers. It sported four antennas—three regular ones and a special white cone-shaped device on the trunk that communicated with earth-orbiting satellites to help determine the car's position. Part of what made the car "smart" was TravTek, a high-technology operation designed to help even the most seriously lost driver get from one place to another.

To use TravTek, the driver entered a destination into the computer, which determined the best route and displayed it on a color monitor mounted on the dashboard. Yellow dots flashed on the screen to warn of traffic jams, and a male voice, generated by the computer and amplified through the dashboard, acted as a navigator. Digital transmissions kept the on-board computers up to date at all times by constantly feeding in the latest information on anything that might affect the route.

The "smart car" is still experimental. But the computers, microcontrollers, sensors, and other forms of technology used in it are expected to be a part of most automobiles in the near future. Chances are good that five years from now, for example, a car will be available that sounds an alarm when it comes too close to another car or is in any other position that might end in a collision. Ten years from now, drivers will probably be able to get on a highway and put the car on autopilot to do the driving while they stretch out and take a nap, read a book.

Other changes are expected as well in the next few years. Chips in the music system will adjust the volume of a car radio, cassette player, or compact disk, taking into account outside noise. When a driver tries to back up, rear radar will warn him or her if an obstacle is in the way. Nor will drivers have as many buttons or knobs to work as they do now because they will be able to control many functions with their voice.

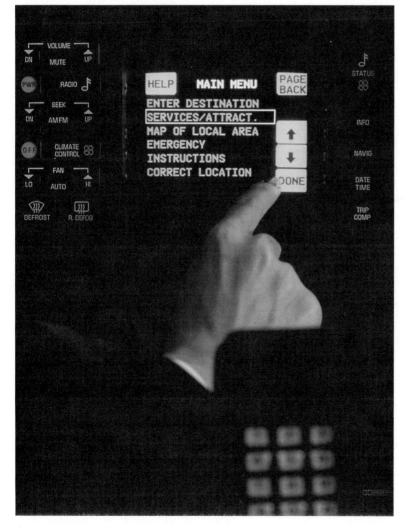

TravTek's on-board computers give the driver information about location, destination, routes, and drive times.

A TravTek map (above) provides a driver with route information on a touch-screen display mounted in the dashboard of a specially equipped Oldsmobile Toronado (left).

The cellular phone and the sound systems in the car will be integrated, so when the driver picks up the car phone, the volume of whatever is playing on the sound system will automatically lower. Even highways will become "smart" after the turn of the century. The "smart" highway will take control of vehicles if there is congestion, automatically controlling the flow of traffic and preventing speeding and accidents.

People are already planning for changes for future decades. No one can say for sure exactly what the car of the future will be like. But there can be no argument with the electronics expert who proclaimed that the car "is becoming a computer on wheels."

Glossary

acid rain: Rainwater that contains pollutants and toxic industrial waste.

assembly line: A system under which individual workers perform specific tasks in putting together a product as the incomplete item passes from one worker to another on a slowly moving belt or track.

automobile: A self-propelled land vehicle, usually with four wheels.

axle: The metal supporting rod on which wheels revolve.

carburetor: A device that mixes air with fuel and feeds the mixture into the cylinders of an internal combustion gasoline engine.

chassis: The basic metal framework of an automobile.

crank: A device used to start or operate early automobiles.

cylinder: A short, broad, tubular chamber in the engine in which a piston moves up and down.

disk brakes: A set of four metal disks, one revolving with each wheel, that functions as brakes when pressure is applied to the friction pads that sandwich each disk.

ethanol: Ethyl alcohol.

exhaust: Fumes and gases that escape from the engine and are released into the air.

flywheel: A heavy, solid wheel that helps make the engine run smoothly at low speeds.

four-stroke engine: An internal combustion engine in which the power stroke—downward plunge of the piston—occurs once for every four times the piston goes up and down.

fuel injection: A system used in some engines instead of a carburetor to supply fuel to the cylinders by injection.

gasohol: A fuel consisting of a blend of about 90 percent unleaded gasoline and 10 percent alcohol.

interchangeable parts: Identical parts that can be quickly assembled to manufacture a product or to replace broken parts.

internal combustion engine: An engine in which a mixture of air and fuel is compressed inside a cylinder and ignited by a spark plug.

magneto: A small generator used in the ignition systems of some internal combustion engines.

mass production: Manufacturing of goods in large quantities.

piston: A plunger that moves up and down in a cylinder.

rotary engine: An engine in which fuel energy is converted directly into rotary, or turning, movements.

sedan: A closed automobile with two or four doors and front and rear seats that generally accommodate at least four people

smog: Fog mixed and polluted with smoke.

spark plug: The element that creates the electric spark that ignites the fuel-air mixture in the cylinders of an internal combustion engine.

streamlining: The designing of the shape of an automobile in such a way as to reduce wind resistance.

supercharger: A blower or compressor that supplies air under high pressure to the cylinders of an internal combustion engine to increase engine power.

suspension: The system of springs and other devices that cushions the impact to jolts and bumps caused by a rough roadway.

tiller: A lever used to steer a vehicle.

transmission: A group of gears and parts that transmits power from the engine to a driving axle or shaft.

turbine: Engine.

two-stroke engine: An internal combustion engine in which the power stroke—downward plunge of the piston—occurs once for every two times the piston goes up and down.

valve: A mechanism that regulates the flow of a gas or liquid through an opening.

vanadium: An element that, when alloyed with steel, gives a metal that is stronger, harder, and more stable at higher temperatures than steel.

For Further Reading

James P. Barry, *Ford and Mass Production.* New York: Franklin Watts, 1973.

Gordon Cruikshank, *Cars and How They Work.* New York: Dorling Kindersley, 1992.

Editors of the Saturday Evening Post, *The Automobile Book.* Indianapolis, IN: Curtis, 1977.

Barbara Ford, *The Automobile.* New York: Walker, 1987.

Ross R. Olney, *Car of the Future.* Hillsdale, NJ: Enslow Publishers, 1986.

Peter Roberts, *Automobiles of the World.* Chicago: Follett, 1966.

Jonathan P. Rutland, *The Age of Steam.* New York: Random House, 1987.

Jonathan P. Rutland, *The Amazing Fact Book of Cars.* Mankato, MN: Creative Education, 1988.

Richard Sutton, *Car: Eyewitness Books.* New York: Knopf, 1990.

K.C. Tessendorf, *Look Out! Here Comes Stanley Steamer.* New York: Atheneum Press, 1984.

Robert John Wyatt, *Cars.* New York: Grosset & Dunlap, 1971.

Works Consulted

■■■

Books

John Bentley, *Oldtime Steam Cars*. Arco Handi-Books for Better Living. New York: Arco, 1953.

Thea Bergere, *Automobiles of Yesteryear*. New York: Dodd, Mead, 1962.

Floyd Clymer, *Treasury of Early American Automobiles: 1877-1925*. New York: Bonanza Books, 1950.

Frank Donovan, *Wheels for a Nation*. New York: Crowell, 1965.

Editors of Automobile Quarterly, *The American Car Since 1775*. New York: L. Scott Bailey, 1971.

Editors of Automobile Quarterly, *General Motors: The First 75 Years of Transportation Products*. Princeton, NJ: Automobile Quarterly; Detroit: General Motors Corporation, 1983.

Raymond Flower and Michael Wynn Jones, *100 Years on the Road: A Social History of the Car*. New York: McGraw-Hill, 1981.

Karl Ludvigsen and David Burgess Wise, *The Complete Encyclopedia of the American Automobile*. Secaucus, NJ: Chartwell Books, 1979.

National Geographic Special Publications Division, *Those Inventive Americans*. Washington, DC: National Geographic Society, 1971.

Wilfred Owen, Ezra Bowen, and the Editors of Time-Life Books, *Wheels*. Life Science Library. New York: Time-Life Books, 1968.

Vernon Pizer, *The Irrepressible Automobile: A Freewheeling Jaunt Through the Fascinating World of the Motorcar*. New York: Dodd, Mead, 1986.

Cyril Posthumus, *Vintage Cars: Motoring in the 1920s.* London: Hamlyn, 1973.

Ken W. Purdy, *Wonderful World of the Automobile.* New York: Crowell, 1963.

Gary Reyes, *The Automobile: Horseless Carriages to Cars of the Future.* New York: Mallard Press, 1990.

Peter Roberts, *A Picture History of the Automobile.* London: Triune Books, 1973.

Joseph H. Wherry, *Automobiles of the World: The Story of the Development of the Automobile.* Philadelphia: Chilton, 1968.

David Burgess Wise, *Veteran and Vintage Cars.* New York: Grossett & Dunlap, 1971.

Periodicals

Mark Fischetti, "Here Comes the Electric Car— It's Sporty, Aggressive and Clean," *Smithsonian,* April 1992.

Noel Grove, "The Automobile and the American Way: Swing Low, Sweet Chariot," *National Geographic,* July 1983.

Newspapers

William Booth, "The Computer-Driven Car of the Future," *Washington Post National Weekly Edition,* May 25-31, 1992.

Columbus Dispatch, "Chips Fall in Automakers' Direction as Electronics Take Over," March 12, 1993.

Columbus Dispatch, "Detroit Recognizing Benefits of Building Cars That Can Be Recycled," March 12, 1993.

Columbus Dispatch, "Electrics Humming Along," August 3, 1991.

Columbus Dispatch, "Mazda Places Its Clean-Fuel Bet on Hydrogen Power," April 17, 1992.

Columbus Dispatch, "Research Rolling on Self-Guided Vehicles," March 12, 1993.

Lesley Hazleton, "Electric Cars Are Charging Toward the Future," *Columbus Dispatch*, April 5, 1992.

Tom Incantalupo, "Computer Revolution Takes Cars for a Spin," *Columbus Dispatch*, August 3, 1991.

Vince Kowalick, "Time Has Come for Electric Car, Many Believe," *Columbus Dispatch*, June 20, 1991.

Michael Parrish, "Picking Up Steam," *Los Angeles Times*, January 2, 1993.

Betsy Wade, "'Smart' Cars That Navigate," *New York Times*, March 29, 1992.

Index

■■

About the Author

■■

Myra H. Immell did her undergraduate study at Ohio University and at the Universidad de Madrid and her graduate study at Rutgers University. She taught Spanish and English as a Second Language for a number of years. For more than 20 years, she was associated with Merrill Publishing Company, where her primary involvement was with textbooks and other educational materials for the social studies.

For the past several years, Immell has been a free-lance author, editor, and educational consultant. One of her most challenging projects during this time was R.R. Bowker's two-volume reference, *The Young Adult Reader's Adviser*, a work on which she served as general editor.

Picture Credits

■■